DJANGO 3

FOR

BEGINNERS

DEDICATION

Thank you Dominique Zillmann, for broadening my understanding of the world, the true face of the human kind. I had great fun all over Spain. Ah and, bfb nuttöö.

A big thank you goes to my parents, for supporting me in every possible way on every journey.

The most applause goes to me. For being awesome, cute, perfect and very humble. Couldn't have done it without you.

FOREWORD

I'm glad you've made it this far. In this book, you will learn to create a web application with Django 3, a web framework for the Python programming language. You will learn the essential web development concepts and all the necessary information to get started with Django 3. But before Django 3, we will learn the basic concepts of programming and the Programming Language Python 3.9.

We will build a blogging web application with added features. Users will be able to post blogs. The application will also have a feature that allows users to post questions and provide answers to them.

Our blog application will be focused on the theme of finance; that is, our blogs will be focused on finance and how people can improve their finance, do their taxes, tips on savings, etc. Our question/answer section will be focused on finance, as well.

If you note, you can convert this application to any theme you like, i.e., tech, writing, etc. We, however, will be making this blog a website that focuses on finance.

By the end of this book, you'll have enough knowledge in Django 3 and web development, in general, to build web apps on your own. You'll also know how to deploy your Django 3 Application in a Serverless Environment in a Cloud.

ABOUT THIS BOOK

This book is designed to be used both digital and printed. Therefore, I have made plenty of screenshots for people who like to read the book (ebook and printed) without immediately implementing the code. This ensures a smooth and hassle-free reading experience.

If, on the other hand, you want to learn the contents as quickly as possible, you can clone the official GitHub repository and save time. I highly recommend you not to use the GitHub repository at the beginning of this journey, especially if you are new to Django. Type the code symbol by symbol yourself. You can find the Github Repository: https://github.com/AndreyBulezyuk/Django-3-Book.

This ensures that you fail quickly in the beginning and learn about the common pitfalls (like forgetting to execute the migrations, not updating the Entity, etc.). You deprive yourself of this learning opportunity when simply clone the code.

The structure of the content is somewhat different from other programming books. It's a mix of theory and practice – where practice comes first, and the theory bits are injected into the sub-steps. This ensures that you learn the practical and real-world workflow of building a Django Website. And while you are practicing it, you are learning the theory in tiny-sized bits just at the right time. This way, you won't be overwhelmed by the dry theory. I genuinely believe that this format will have the best impact on your learning journey.

Scientific literature has shown that the best way to learn is by doing, so always try to solve the problems at the end of the chapter. If you are having difficulty solving some of them, do not worry – nobody said programming was easy, remember to take a break when you are feeling tired and be sure to go through the example problems and their solutions.

PYTHON 3

INTRODUCTION

This is an Introduction to Python 3, which means we will cover the Basics of Python3 and the basic concepts of programming. **Python 3.9** is the current stable release, which means you will be learning the newest stuff there is.

WHY PYTHON?

Python 3 is easy to learn, it is the fastest growing language in the world, which means it has a large community behind it, it has thousands of different libraries with new ones being added every day, it is widely used for Machine Learning, Cloud Computing, Web Development, Web Scrapping, Desktop Development and pretty much anything you can think of (even Game & App Dev).

Python is an interpreted, object-oriented, high-level programming language. Interpreted means that every python code file is 'ready to go' and does not require any additional steps to run it, object-oriented means that the language is designed with the intent of creating high-level complex abstractions called 'objects'. Python by design is highly readable, that coupled with the large quantity of different libraries and a strong community is what makes it a beginner friendly language.

SYNTAX AND VARIABLES

WHAT IS A VARIABLE

Think of a variable as a name referring to an object. For example, consider you have a dog and you are describing him to a friend, when you say 'Max is a young puppy' Max is just an *identifier* and every time you use the word 'Max' what you are actually thinking of is the dog itself.

```
myDogName = 'Max'
print(myDogName)
myDogName = 'Max'
```

In programming it is exactly the same - when writing 'myDogName' what I actually am referring to is 'Max' - the name of my dog. To see that this is the case we can simply use the 'print' command to retrieve the content of the variable.

BASIC DATA TYPES IN PYTHON

In most programming languages the programmer must specify beforehand what type will the type of data stored in that variable be, the most common of those types are – natural numbers (integers), decimal point numbers (floating point real values) and text (strings).

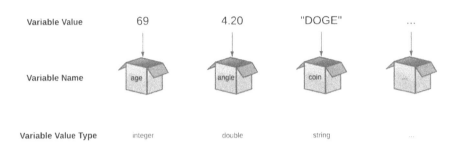

Variable Value	69	4.20	"DOGE"	...
Variable Name	age	angle	coin	...
Variable Value Type	integer	double	string	...

In Python this process is handled automatically and is hidden from the programmer and thus makes the code much easier to read. To see for yourself we will use the built-in *'type()'* function which gives us as a result the underlying type of the variable.

```
myString = "A great day to learn Python"
print(type(myString))

myInt = 42
print(type(myInt))

myFloat = 3.14
print(type(myFloat))
```

VARIABLE MANIPULATION

VARIABLE ASSIGNMENT

This is one of the most fundamental operations you will deal with as a programmer, since if variables are empty boxes, *assigning* a value to them is the act of filling them up. The assignment is done by using the *'equals'* (=) sign. To demonstrate how the assignment operator works and how the data type changes between assignments we will use the *'type'* and *'print' functions* we just discussed in the following example.

```
myVariable = 10
print(type(myVariable))

myVariable = 10.1
print(type(myVariable))

myVariable = "Yes, I can do this"
print(type(myVariable))
```

In this example you can clearly see that variables are *'dynamic'* in nature, that is they do not have a predefined type or property they must adhere to. That is why I am first able to use the variable to hold a natural number, then a float, and then a string.

This leads us to another important aspect of the process of assignment, there are two parts to the assignment the 'Left-Hand Side' and the 'Right-Hand Side' or for short 'LHS' and 'RHS', determined by which side of the equals sign they are situated. The LHS is the variable that is being **assigned to** while the RHS is what is **being assigned**.

In other words, the LHS is the box and the RHS is the data that goes into the box. Note that this is not exactly what is happening underneath the hood, in actuality everything in Python is an object and variable names – *point to* these objects, but for now this is the analogy we will go with.

In the following example you will see that both the RHS and the LHS can be variables and thus our box-data analogy is not very clear, since both sides appear to be boxes. What assignment means in this case is that we want to **copy** the data contained in the RHS and just like before put that copy into the LHS box. Keep in mind copying the contents is not always the case, when we are dealing with objects, but more on that in Chapter Six.

```
A = 1000
B = A    # B is the LHS and A is the RHS
print(B)

C = "My Sentence"
D = C
print(D)

#Note we can overwrite the already
#existing contents of the LHS with assignment
E = "Pizza"
F = "Broccoli"
E = F
print(E)
```

Note that when assigning data values to variables, the variable should **always** be on the left-hand side of the assignment operator. Because data is **not** a variable and thus by our box analogy is not a box and therefore cannot hold data.

```
myVariable = 20
10 = myVariable
#This will result in an error 'Cannot assign to literal'
#Which is very intuitive, since 10 is not a box and doesn't make sense for it to hold
anything
```

This is an example shows what **not** to do, using our previous analogy – variables are the boxes in which we put in our objects(data), thus it does not make sense to try and put anything inside data, because by definition only boxes can contain things.

Another example of what not to do is, assigning a variable that has not been defined yet

```
myVariable = 10
myVariable = somethingNotDefined
#This results in a 'not defined' error, because
#Python cannot evaluate the RHS, since we've never specified what it means
```

In the following example you will see how we can combine our knowledge of the dynamic nature of Python variables and how the assignment operator works.

```
A = 10
B = "Not a number"
A = B
print(type(A))
```

ARITHMETIC EXPRESSIONS

We learned what variables are, their types and how to assign them. Now we will focus on the numeric types of data and how create arithmetic expressions, just like we learned in school.

```
a = 10
b = 20
c = a + b
print(c)
```

Note that even though in this case the result is the same, arithmetic expressions in programming are not the same as solving mathematical equations, thus it is best not to think of the above example as finding the unknown variable – c, but more in terms of what we discussed in the previous paragraph – LHS is the variable to which we will assign the result of the RHS expression. If we keep this in mind the principles are the same as previously discussed and we will focus on evaluating the RHS expression.

We will discuss and show examples of the classic mathematical operators – addition, subtraction, multiplication, and division.

```
print(50+10)
print(50-10)
print(50*10)
print(50/10)
```

Everything works as you would expect it to, each of them is binary which means it needs two variables or pieces of data – called *operands*. The subtraction operator can also be unary, meaning it can take a single operand, that is the operation called – negation. Also, it is worth noting that when calling the division operator regardless if the result is a whole number, the type of the result is always '*float*', when a variable is of type float even though it's a whole number Python displays the number as 10.0 to remind you of it.

```
myVariable = 100
print(-myVariable)

floatExperiment = myVariable/10
print(type(floatExperiment))
```

There are three other operators beside the classical ones – exponentiation, modulo, and floor division.

```
print(2**10) #Exponentiation

moduloDivision = 999%100
print(moduloDivision)

floorDivision = 999//100
print(floorDivision)
print(type(floorDivision)) #Floor Division
```

The first operand in exponentiation Is the base number and the second operand is its power, hence 2 to the power of 10 is 1024. Modulo Division is the act of taking the remainder of the division of the first operand by the second operand. Floor division on the other hand acts the same way as ordinary division, but it always rounds down to an integer value, so in other words – division without remainder.

Another aspect of arithmetic expressions is the problem of operator precedence, just like in mathematics division and multiplication have a higher priority than addition and subtraction, additionally exponentiation has the highest precedence of them.

If we want to enforce a specific order of operations, just like in math class – we use brackets and if you are not certain on which operator takes precedence it is always a good practice to use brackets.

```
noBrackets = 1000/10+50
print(noBrackets)

withBrackets = 1000/(10+50)
print(withBrackets)
```

Note that the same problems outlined in the previous paragraph apply here and for any future chapters as well. Using not defined variables will result in an error.

```
A = 10
B = 20
C = 100
Result = A + B + C + Z    # Z is not defined
print(Result)
```

This will be a common theme in this book, so make sure you think about how what we have previously learned can be applied to what we are currently learning as this is the basis of advanced programming.

VARIABLE NAMES

There are four rules to which every Python variable name must adhere to:

- A variable name must start with a letter or the underscore character
- A variable name can only contain alpha-numeric characters and underscores
- Variable names are case-sensitive (git, Git and GIT are three different variable names)
- Keywords cannot be used as variable names

Keywords are reserved words which cannot be used as variable or function names, each of them serves a specific purpose and using the keyword invokes a certain behavior from Python. Examples of keywords are: if, elif, else, def, import, False, True, del, break, continue, for, from, while etc.

The following example lists valid and invalid variable names in Python

```
#Valid variable names:
myvar = "GitAcademy"
my_var = "GitAcademy"
_my_var_ = "GitAcademy"
myVar = "GitAcademy"
MYVAR = "GitAcademy"
my42var = "GitAcademy"
MY999__VAR_999 = "GitAcadmy"

#Invalid variable names:
my-var = "GitAcademy"
9myvar = "GitAcademy"
my var = "GitAcademy"
continue = "GitAcademy"
```

DATA TYPES IN PYTHON

LIST

A list is a collection of objects. Lists are characterized for being:

- Ordered – items in the list have an order that does not change
- Changeable – We can change, add, and remove items in the list
- Allows Duplicates – We can have more than one item with the same value

A list is a collection of objects enclosed by square brackets

```python
myLetters = ['a','b','c','d']
print(myLetters)
```

Note that with Lists we can hold values and variables of different types, so an expression like this is completely valid

```python
myVariable = 'Variable'

myList = [1, -1, 3.14, 'GitAcademy', myVariable]
print(myList)
```

TUPLE

Tuples are collections of data that can hold multiple items in a single variable. Tuples are characterized for being:

- Ordered – items in the list have an order that does not change
- Unchangeable – After creating the tuple we cannot modify its contents
- Allows Duplicates – We can have more than one item with the same value

A tuple is a collection of objects enclosed by curved brackets

```
myTuple = (1,-1,3.14,'GitAcademy')
```

Notice that we can use variables when defining our tuple, however once the tuple is defined all of its member objects are **immutable** – meaning unchangeable.

```
myFloat = 3.14
myString = 'Some String Data'

myTuple = (myString, myFloat)
print(myTuple)
```

SET

Sets, similarly to tuples are collections of data that can hold multiple items in a single variable. Sets are characterized for being:

- Unordered – items in the set do not have an order
- Unchangeable – After creating the set we cannot modify its contents
- Duplicates Not Allowed – Sets cannot have two items with the same value

A set is a collection of objects enclosed by curly brackets

```
myVariable = 'GitAcademy'

mySet = {1, -1, 3.14, 'Joe', myVariable}
print(mySet)
```

Notice that running the first example numerous times, displays the members of the set in a different order – that is a direct cause of the collection being 'unordered'.

In the following example take note of the third property of sets – not allowing any duplicates. In this case the contents of *myVariable* are *GitAcademy* and I have entered *GitAcademy* as a string literal a second time.

```
myVariable = 'GitAcademy'

mySet = {'GitAcademy', myVariable, 3.14}
print(mySet)
```

As expected, the resulting tuple contains *GitAcademy* only once.

DICTIONARY

A dictionary is a collection of key: value pairs. Dictionaries are characterized for being:

- Unordered – items in the dictionary do not have an order
- Changeable – We can change, add, and remove items in a dictionary
- Duplicates Not Allowed – Dictionaries cannot have two items with the same value

I will only demonstrate how a dictionary looks like in order to frontload the concept, however do not worry about how they work exactly as we will discuss that in the following segment.

```
myDictionary = {
    'Year Of Graduation': 2020,
    'Final Grade': 10.0,
    'Name of Student': 'John Doe',
}

print(myDictionary['Name of Student'])
```

DATA-TYPE METHODS

As the name suggests data-type methods are methods(functions) that are specific to a certain data type. They make it possible for us to interact with these objects in many different ways, most common of which are – adding elements, removing elements and searching for elements.

First of all, we should note that the '.'(dot) operator is used to access class members that are defined for that object. The class is the template for the object and class members can be variables and functions. For now, do not worry too much about it, we will discuss at length what exactly does that mean in Chapter Seven, for now we just need a working understanding of the concept – that is, every time we use the dot operator, we are accessing a member of the object.

LIST METHODS

List are quite likely the most used type for collections of objects and this is why it is very important to build a solid understanding of how to manipulate them, since as of now the different collections of objects we introduced, seem somewhat static and dull. Worry not, when we get through what data-type methods are and how to use them you will gain an appreciation for the complexity they allow for and the elegant ways in which they can be used for problem-solving.

Consider this introductory paragraph as a way for the author to stress how important the following segment will be for a proper introduction into Python. Unless you are already confident in these concepts consider revisiting this section at least a few times.

As of now we learned how to define different collections of objects and what their properties are. Now we will introduce methods to interact with lists, first and foremost we will explain the list append method that will allow us to add new items into the list.

RETRIEVE BY INDEX

Since lists are ordered, that means we can index them. The act of indexing means that we can retrieve an element from a list using its index number. The index number tells us how many elements after the first one, our element is situated at, so an index number of 1 means that this is the second element (remember that in programming counting always begins from 0). An index number of 5 means this is the sixth number and so on and so forth.

I will take this as an opportunity to mention the *'len()'* method which returns the number of elements in the collection. If we have an empty list – len() would yield the number zero. If we have 3 elements in the list – len() will yield the number 3 and in general If we have n elements in the collection len() will give us the number n.

LEN()

```
myList = ['Orange','Apple','Banana']
print(len(myList))
print(myList[5])
```

We define the list in the same way as previously discussed. When using the *'len()'* function we see it returns the number 3, which is exactly the number of elements in the list. Indexing the list is done with the notation used in the second print statement, we can see that retrieving an item at an index is done by using the variable name immediately followed by square brackets containing the index number.

Note that if we use an index number that is larger than the number of elements minus one (since we are counting from zero) we will get a 'index out of range' error and the program will not run.

APPEND()

Instead of retrieving an item in the collection – appending is the act of adding one new item **at the end** of the list.

```
myList = ['Orange','Apple','Banana']
print(len(myList))
myList.append('Chocolate Bar')
listLength = len(myList)
print(listLength)
print(myList[listLength-1])
```

In this code snippet we are using the same list as in the previous example and we want to add another item to it. To do that we use the *append()* class method (I am specifying it is a class method since you cannot append items to a tuple for example – it is specific to objects of type list).

After we execute the append command, we save the result of the *len()* command into a variable. When printing the same variable, we can now clearly see that the number of objects in the list has increased by one which is indeed what happened.

We can now use retrieval by index to print out our newest addition to our collection. As we previously mentioned – the appended item goes to the back of our list, so to retrieve it we used the last index which is the length of the list minus one (because the first item is with an index of zero).

INSERT()

The insert command is similar to append with the added caveat of us being able to specify at which index do we want to add a new object to the list. The insert method takes in two parameters, the first one being the index at which we would want to insert our new object in the collection and the second one being the object itself.

```python
myList = ['Orange','Apple','Banana']
print(myList[0])
myList.insert(0,'Chocolate Bar')
print(myList[0])
```

Here we inserted our newest object at the first index – meaning the front of the list. As you can see after the insertion when we retrieve the first object it is indeed the object we just added. This implies the natural consequence that when we insert an object at the *I-th* index the indices of all objects after the *I-th* index will increase their index by one, while the indices of the objects before the insertion index will remain the same.

POP()

In the same way we used append and insert to add new entries into our collection – now we can remove items with the pop method. *Pop()* takes in a single argument – the index of the item we would like to remove.

```python
myList = ['Orange','Apple','Banana']
print(myList[0])
myList.pop(0)
print(len(myList))
print(myList[0])
```

Using the same example, we can verify that the first item in the collection is indeed 'Orange' and as you might expect when we pop the element at the first index (which is specified by the number zero) the length of the list shrinks by one and the new first item is our previously second item.

Again, the same principle applies as with insertion, but in reverse – when we delete the *I-th* item from the list the indices of all subsequent items are reduced by one, while the indices of items before the item we have removed remain unchanged.

SET METHODS

The concept of a set first arose in the field of mathematics and operations with sets are fundamentally mathematical. The defining feature of a set is that it is both unordered and does not allow duplicates. Which implies that all elements in the set share a similar property (hence why they are in the same set).

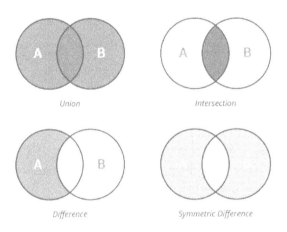

Union

Intersection

Difference

Symmetric Difference

ADD()

The add method is used to add another object to the set, it takes in a single parameter – the object to be added.

```
expensivePets = {'Parrots','Monkeys','Tigers','Lions'}
expensivePets.add('Tigers')
print(expensivePets)
```

In this example you can see a set of items – in this case animals, which share the common property of being expensive. It just so happens that we add an animal that was already in the set. As expected, the updated set remains the same as 'Tigers' were already in the set of expensive animals. It is important to understand why this is the case. If we think of the set as a collection of objects sharing the same property it does not make sense to add 'Tigers' a second time to the set since an object can either have or not have a certain property.

INTERSECTION()

Intersection is a method of a set that takes in any number of sets as its parameters. If as previously discussed, sets contain elements with the same property, then an intersection of sets is a set containing the elements that satisfy all of the properties.

```
expensivePets = {'Parrots','Monkeys','Tigers','Lions'}
dangerousAnimals = {'Lions','Tigers','Hyennas','Rhinos'}
dangerousPets = expensivePets.intersection(dangerousAnimals)
print(dangerousPets)
```

In this example we have our previous set of expensive pets and another set of dangerous animals and we make the observation that expensive pets that are dangerous animals are indeed dangerous pets to own.

That is exactly what we achieve by using the intersection method. When we call the intersection method it takes only the common elements to all sets. Which if properly labeled are animals that are both expensive and dangerous.

```
expensivePets = {'Parrots','Monkeys','Tigers','Lions'}
dangerousAnimals = {'Lions','Tigers','Hyennas','Rhinos'}
dangerousPets = dangerousAnimals.intersection(expensivePets)
print(dangerousPets)
```

Notice that this is exactly the same example, however we have called the intersection method from the other set and the result remains the same. This is so, because taking the common elements of several sets is a commutative operation – that is, it does not matter what the order of operations is – just like with addition 7 + 5 = 5 + 7.

UNION()

Similarly, to the intersection method – union takes any number of sets as parameters. Continuing with the notion that sets are collections of objects with the same property – the union method returns a set that contains all of the elements from all sets. So, in a sense it is the dual operation of intersection.

```
lowNumbers = {1, 2, 3 ,4, 5, 6}
highNumbers = {4, 5, 6, 7, 8, 9}
allNumbers = lowNumbers.union(highNumbers)
print(allNumbers)
commonNumbers = lowNumbers.intersection(highNumbers)
print(commonNumbers)
```

In this example you can see that the resulting set has all the numbers from the low numbers set and all of the numbers from the high numbers set. Again, the union method is commutative, so it does not matter in what order we take the union of the sets. Below I have provided as an example how the intersection of both sets would look like.

DICTIONARY METHODS

Dictionaries are a collection of key value pairs, where each key refers to a specific value. The role of the key is identical of that of the index in lists. The key is said to 'point' to its respective value. When we access a specific key in our dictionary it returns us the value to which it points.

ACCESSING DICTIONARY VALUES

```
studentRecord = {
    'Graduation Year': 2020,
    'Grade': 10.0,
    'Name': 'John Doe',
    'Country': 'Germany',
}

print(studentRecord['Name'])
```

The notation is exactly the same as when we retrieved values with indices when we learned about list methods. The difference here is that dictionaries are unordered, thus we cannot simply state that we would like to retrieve the second element of the collection. However, we have a notion for keys, which play the role of the index. If this was a list and we wanted to access the third element we would say *studentRecord[2]*, instead here we use the key '*Name*' which maps to its respective value.

ADDING NEW KEY-VALUE PAIRS

Doing this is very intuitive, so much so, you might not realize you are doing it.

```
studentRecord = {
    'Graduation Year': 2020,
    'Grade': 10.0,
    'Name': 'John Doe',
    'Country': 'Germany',
}

studentRecord['Honors Student'] = True
print(studentRecord['Honors Student'])
```

Using the same example, we decide that we want to have an additional field in our student record called 'Honors Student', in order for that to happen all we need to do is to remember the exact syntax or variable assignment and apply it in the same way as shown in the example.

What happens is that we assign a new value to a new key. Sure enough, when we check for the contents of the new key the data is there. Note that the syntax for changing the value of an already existing key is exactly the same.

DATA TYPECASTING

In the opening paragraph of this chapter, we briefly discussed the different types of variables and how Python automatically handles this for us. That is not always to our advantage and we sometimes need the behavior of a specific data type.

```
myVariable = '3.14'
print(type(myVariable))

myVariable = float(myVariable)
print(myVariable + 100)

print(type(myVariable))
```

In this example we have a variable of type string which we use the float() command to cast to the type of float, which we can which allows us to make use of the expected functionality of a float number.

```
myVariable = '1'
secondVariable = '2'
print(myVariable + secondVariable)

print(int(myVariable)+int(secondVariable))
```

In the second example you can see that the default behavior of the addition operator (+) is to concatenate strings, so if we want to use it in the sense of adding numbers, we have to tell that to Python explicitly by using the int() command.

USER INPUT

So far, we have learned a lot about different data types and their behavior however everything is rather static and unchanging. Now we are about to change that by learning to read user input.

```
myName = input("Enter your name: ")
print ("Hello,", myName)
```

To prompt the user to enter something all you need to do is call the input function and optionally pass a message to the user as a parameter. The input function is the right-hand side of an assignment operator and the input is stored in the left-hand side.

```
myNumber = input("Please enter a number: ")
print(type(myNumber))
myNumber = int(myNumber)
print("This is the number squared:",myNumber**2)
```

A key point to remember is that the input function always returns a string object. It is very important to cast your input to the expected variable type so as to avoid unexpected behavior in your program.

```
listOfFoods = input("Enter your favorite foods separated by a space: \n").split()
print(listOfFoods)
```

In this example we introduce the split method– which we use on top of the input method in order to separate the items from our input in a list. If we were to not use the split method, we would end up with a string that contains the entire input. You can try this for yourself by removing split.

CONDITIONAL EXPRESSIONS

WHAT IS A CONDITIONAL EXPRESSION?

A conditional expression is a computer science paradigm common to all programming languages. The idea is that we want to check if a certain condition is present and then act upon it. It may sound somewhat abstract so let me give you a real-world example – imagine you are about to go to school when you see that it is raining outside.

You think to yourself – **if** it is raining **then** I will take an umbrella with me. Is it raining or not is the condition we want to evaluate and taking the umbrella is the action we would perform. This is what is called a block diagram. This block diagram specifically represents the logical flow of an 'if statement'. The black dot at the top Is the entry point for our program and the flow of the program is given by the direction of the arrows.

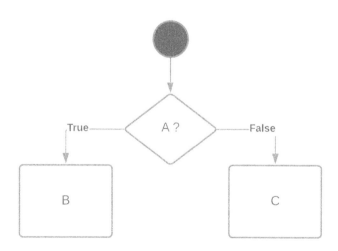

In this example – the program starts. We check if the condition A is true or not. If it is true, we continue acting out B, and if it is not, we act out C. The program ends.

In the terms of our example this would be interpreted the following way:

- Condition: A – Is it raining?
  - Consequence: B – Take umbrella
  - Consequence: C – Continue as usual

Note that this may be a little confusing as this mysterious C is not defined in our example, but bear with me for a few more examples and I promise we will get to that.

WHAT IS A LOGICAL EXPRESSION?

We will make a detour to discuss how to express the condition of our 'if statement'. The condition is what is called a logical expression. Logical expressions are formulas (expressions) that evaluate to true or false. So, for the purposes of this tutorial, you can consider everything that can be answer by either true, or false – as a logical expression.

LOGICAL COMPARISON

Previously, we used the equals sign to assign the right-hand side to the left-hand side. If, however, we use the equals sign twice in a row – that means we want to compare if the right-hand side is equal to the left-hand side. Note that when it comes to comparisons the left-hand side and the right-hand side have the same purpose and therefore properties, unlike with assignment.

```
A = 10
B = 20
C = 10

print(A == B)
print(A == C)
```

As discussed – the result of a logical expressions is always True or False, depending if the expression is... well True or False. Another type of logical comparison is lesser/greater than.

```
A = 10
B = 20
C = 10

print(A < B)
print(A < C)
```

Surely enough, the result is again True/False. The idea is the same as with comparing if two values are equal. Here we compare if the left-hand side is lesser than the right-hand side. Note that it is a strict comparison – the lhs number has to be strictly lesser than the rhs number. The greater than operator works in the exact same way, so I will leave it up to you to experiment with.

If we do not want a strict comparison then we will use the lesser-than-or-equal or greater-than-or-equal operators, which, as you probably suspect – work in the exact same way as their strict counterparts.

```
A = 10
B = 20
C = 10

print(A <= B)
print(A <= C)
```

LOGICAL OPERATOR: AND

Now that we discussed how to do logical comparisons, we will learn how to build complex logical statements.

Imagine we want to know if a number is in the range of 1 and 100, unfortunately there is no operator that can do this for us, so we will have to do it ourselves. The logical **and** operator takes two logical expressions outputs True only when all of the expressions evaluate to True. To do that we use the keyword **and**

```
X = float(input("Enter a number: "))
answer = 1 < X and X < 100
print(answer)
```

When the number is between 1 and 100 both of the expressions evaluate to True. However, if it is above 100 or below 1 one expression evaluates to True, but the other evaluates to False which is all that 'and' needs to return a False answer.

LOGICAL OPERATOR: OR

As with logical and – logical or is used to build complex logical statements, by taking in two logical expressions and returning True when at least one of the expressions evaluates to True and returns False only when both of the expressions are false.

In this problem statement we want to find out if the multiplication of two numbers will result in an even number, without multiplying them.

```
A = int(input("Enter A: "))
B = int(input("Enter B: "))

answer = A%2==0 or B%2==0

print(answer)
```

Okay, so this example may be a little more convoluted so let me explain. A number is even when it is divisible by two. When multiplying two numbers if either of them is divisible by two, then the resulting number will also be divisible by two. That is exactly what our program statement is saying – if A is divisible by two **or** if B is divisible by two then the result will be divisible by two. All that is required for the result to be divisible by two is if **either** A or B be divisible by two.

LOGICAL OPERATOR: NOT

Logical Not is similar to and/or, that it modifies in some manner an already logical expression. The difference is that it takes in only a single expression and inverts it. Not True would mean False and Not False would mean True. So, if we go with the problem where we check if a number is between 1 and 100 and add the not operator, the result will be True only when the number is **not** in the interval 1-100.

```
X = float(input("Enter a number: "))
answer = not(1 < X and X < 100)
print(answer)
```

CODE BLOCKS

When writing an if statement we want to execute a bunch of commands if some criteria is met. But how does Python know which statements are part of the commands to be executed inside the if statement and which are not? That is by using code blocks here is an example in C++.

```cpp
#include <iostream>
int main(void)
{
    int X = 42;
    if (X == 42) {  //This is a code block
        X = 1;
        X = 2;
        X = 3;
        //...
        X = 100;
    } //No statements after this
      //will be part of the if statement
    X = 101;
    return 0;
}
```

As you can see, we are doing multiple assignments inside the if statements and the curly braces help the C++ compiler understand which statements belong inside the if statements and which do not.

The same principle applies to all programming languages. In Python, however, there are no braces to denote this, just the ':' symbol and a consistent indentation.

```python
if False:
    print("Hi")
    print("Hi")
    #...
    print("Hi")

print("Hi")
```

Because the condition always evaluates to False, the insides of the if statements will never be read or reached. However, the syntax is correct, and the program runs seamlessly. You can try and change the indentation and see for yourself that Python will throw you an error.

IF STATEMENTS

Finally, we are going to talk about if statements. Before I continue with our first example, I just want to mention that mastering conditional expressions is a necessary part for any programmer. It is an essential tool, which forms the basis of loops and of other aspects of programming you will encounter further down the line.

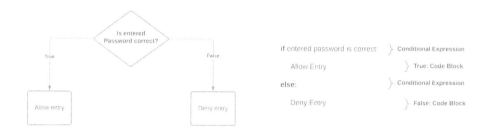

Now to the example – We prompt the user to input his exam score. We do not know ahead of time anything about his score, but we want the program to tell us in plain English if the user has passed the exam. Here is the implementation.

```
myScore = int(input("Enter your exam score(1-100): "))
if myScore >= 70:
    print("You have successfuly passed the course!")
```

You can see that the condition for passing the course is having a score higher or equal than 70. Let us do another example. In this case the user inputs his score and we want to check if his score is a valid score.

```
myScore = int(input("Input your score(1-100): "))
if 1 < myScore or myScore > 100:
    print("You have entered an incorrect score!")
```

We will take this as an opportunity to practice conditional expressions as well. I challenge you to modify this code so that it prints "You have entered a correct score" only when the score is between 1 and 100.

ELSE AND ELIF CLAUSES

So far, we explored what happens when the condition of our if expression is met, the natural extension of that is to consider what to do if the condition is false. If we consider the previous examples where we wanted to check if the entered score is valid, we can rewrite it as follows:

```
myScore = int(input("Input your score(1-100): "))
if 1 <= myScore and myScore <= 100:
    print("The score is valid")
else:
    print("You have entered an incorrect score!")
```

The reason this works and we do not need to specify a condition in front of the else clause is because logical expressions always evaluate to either true or false. Meaning that there are exactly two possibilities for our if statement – for the condition to evaluate to true and for us to enter the if code-block or for the condition to evaluate to false and for us to enter the else code-block. There is no third option – except for the Python Executor to fail (e.g.: when **myScore** is being set to a string instead of integer).

Let us remodel one of our previous examples, if we have passed the test or not.

42

```
myScore = int(input("Enter your exam score(1-100): "))
if myScore >= 70:
    print("You have successfuly passed the course!")
else:
    print("You have failed the course!")
```

The logic is the same as in the previous example – we check if the score is 70 or more and if it is the program issues the corresponding message, however if it is not – we enter the else clause.

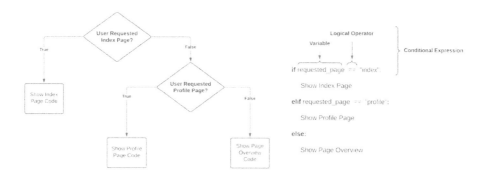

Let us consider another case – a combination of our previous examples. First, we want to validate our score and then we want to check if the student passes or not.

```
myScore = int(input("Input your score(1-100): "))

if 1 > myScore or myScore > 100:
    print("You have entered an incorrect score!")
elif myScore >= 70:
    print("You have successfuly passed the course!")
else:
    print("You have failed the course!")
```

The 'elif' clause is a concatenation of the keywords 'else' and 'if'. It would not make any difference if we were to just write another if clause inside the else of the primary if statement. And thus you would create a nested if-statement. You can consider this a convenience developed, because of the wide use of these types of expressions.

I will present you with a slightly more complex example to illustrate how nested if-statements are used. We are asked to write a survey tracking customer satisfaction with our online product. In order to do so we ask our clients to rate our product and if the rating is not great, we ask them are they satisfied with the product, if they are, we thank them, if not, we ask them why they are not satisfied.

```
score = int(input("Please rate our service (1-5) stars: "))
if score < 1 or score > 5:
    print("You have entered an invalid score.")
elif score <=3:
    feedback = input("Are you satisfied with our service? y/n\n")
    if feedback == 'y':
        print("Thank you for your feedback!")
    elif feedback == 'n':
        moreFeedback = input("What should we do to improve our service?\n")
        print("Thank you for your feedback!")
else:
    print("Thank you for your awesome review!")
```

Having this much code makes it harder to read, this is why indentation comes in handy in order for you to orient yourself as to which code block does this statement belong to.

PROGRAMMING LOOPS

I gave you an early warning that complexity is going to ramp up quickly by the time we touch programing loops and here we are. I hope by now you are somewhat comfortable with logical statements and conditional expressions, because they are a building block to the programming loop.

INTRODUCTION

A loop is a code segment which we would like to execute multiple times, usually changing the state of that code segment with each execution. If we had a number and we wanted to find out if the same number can be found in a list with 10 numbers, we would have to write 10 if statements – now that is not very elegant, but it is still doable. However if the list of numbers is determined at runtime by the users input it would be an impossible task. There is no way for the programmer to know ahead of time how many if statements to write. It is because of these kinds of problems that loops exist.

FOR LOOPS

ITERATORS

Before we get into for loops, we have to cover the concept of iterators. Any Python object that is iterable – which can return one element at a time can have an iterator. The iterator itself is the current element that is being returned. A lot of the Python objects implement the iterator protocol – such as lists, tuples, strings etc.

```
myList = ['apple','orange','pear']
myIter = iter(myList)
print(next(myIter))
print(next(myIter))
print(next(myIter))
```

We have a list of items, and in order to iterate through them we first create the iterator object and call its built-in function 'next' which does exactly that – goes to the next item in the iterated object. Note that if at the end I called 'next' one more time we would go outside the bounds of the iterated object and throw a 'StopIterration' Exception. We will not go into much detail as this is only a stepping stone to our actual subject – for loops.

ORDINARY FOR LOOP

The problem statement is the following – we have an iterable object, for instance say – a list. We want to do some manipulation of that list elementwise.

This is the logical flow of our program. At the beginning we create or fetch (e.g. from a Database) our iterable object. Then we check our condition (have we reached the end of the object) and if not, we enter the body of the for loop. We do that until we reach the end of the object at which point, we continue executing the rest of the program.

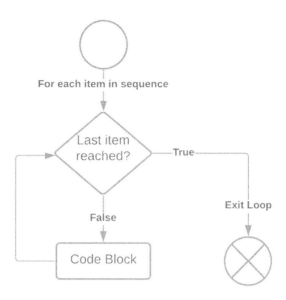

Using the same example as with the iterators, but now with for loops. fruit is our iterator and for each cycle through our loop we implicitly call the 'next' function. Unsurprisingly the result is the same. Let us do another example.

```
for number in range(20):
    print(number)
```

Here we use the very useful 'range' function. With it – what we are saying in essence is – loop through all the numbers from 0 to N. This time, let us try and compute the sum of all numbers from 1 to 100.

```
sum = 0
for number in range(1,101):
    sum = sum + number
print(sum)
```

We used the variable **sum** to accumulate the sum of the numbers through the loop. Notice that we initialized the variable to 0 before entering the loop. Otherwise, Python would not know which variable we are referring to and if we were to declare sum = 0 inside the scope of the **for** loop, then we would effectively set **sum** to zero after each iteration. That would not work either.

We also used **range()** with two arguments, what is that about? Well, the first argument is the number from which we start counting, the second is the number up until which we will count and I will even tell you a secret – there is a third possible argument for range. The third argument is specifying the increment to increase our iterable (it is 1 by default).

Notice also, that in order to sum the numbers from 1 to 100 – I had to call range (1,101) that is, because when the iterator reaches the final value – 101, we exit the for loop.

```
myInput = input("Enter numbers from 0 to 100\n").split()
result = []
for x in myInput:
    if float(x) <= 100 and float(x)>=0:
        result.append(float(x)/100)
print(result)
```

In this example we take the numbers that the user inputs and of those that are between 0-100 we add them to a new list compressed in the range of 0-1. Notice that we need to cast the iterator, since by default anything that reads user input is a string. Notice that the if statement is applied to each item in the list.

```
even = []
odd = []
for x in range(101):
    if x%2==0:
        even.append(x)
    else:
        odd.append(x)

print(even)
print(odd)
```

Here we take the numbers from 0-100 and split them into two lists – those of the even numbers, and those of the odd ones. Take note of the use of indentation to specify which statement belongs to which code block.

WHILE LOOPS

While loops are a more general category of loops.

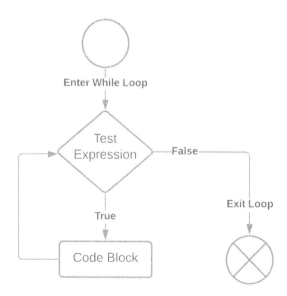

The rhomboid specifies a conditional expression. In for loops our conditional expression was – Have we reached the last item of the iterable object? With while loops it can be any expression.

Since it is a more general expression it means that we can imitate the logical flow of a for expression.

```
x = 0
while x < 11:
    print(x)
    x = x + 1
```

Instead of using the range function, we just imitated its logic by creating our own variable x, told Python we want to execute the statement within the while scope until x is 101 or larger and in effect – we achieved the same result. This also allows us to create a logical flow that cannot be done with a for loop.

Consider we want to create a program that reads random numbers until a specific number is read. We cannot do this with a for loop, because we just do not know how many iterations it will take us for this number to come up, however if we are to use a while expression it is extremely intuitive.

```
from random import randrange

desiredNumber = 42
numberOfCycles = 0
x = randrange(100)

while x != desiredNumber:
    x = randrange(100)
    numberOfCycles = numberOfCycles + 1

print("We found our number in " + str(numberOfCycles) + " iterations!")
```

Here we use a function from the 'random' library called randrange – which generates a random number in the specified range – in our case from 0-100. We do not know ahead of time how many times the loop should be executed which should indicate to you that a while loop is necessary.

You may have noticed however that if our desired number is outside the range in which we generate numbers (say we wanted the number 200) we would never exit the while loop, and this would freeze our entire program. This is why, even though while loops are more powerful, we use them only when necessary, because they can cause infinite loops, out of bounds exceptions, etc. These issues are handled by design in for loops.

```python
x = int(input("Enter a number:\n"))
print(x)
while x != 1:
    if x%2 == 0:
        x = x//2
    else:
        x = 3*x + 1
    print(x, end=" ")
print(x)
```

This example is a famous unsolved mathematical problem called the Collatz Conjecture, solving it will earn you 1,000,000 USD you can look up Wikipedia for more information on the problem, simply put we enter a number and apply the following function to it: if x is even, we divide it by two, if x is odd, we multiply it by 3 and add 1.

Now the question that the conjecture tries to answer is – do we always reach 1 in the end? Now this is yet to be proven hence why it's an unsolved problem, but for all practical purposes we can consider it to be true, since computers have verified it does reach one, up to very large initial numbers, however if it turns out to be false then that would mean that there is some number which when entered will not produce 1 at the end, meaning our while loop will be infinite, which again goes to show how dangerous while loops can be.

```
meals = []
userInput = input("Enter a meal you enjoy ('done' to quit)\n")
while userInput != 'done':
    meals.append(userInput)
    userInput = input("Enter a meal you enjoy ('done' to quit)\n")
print(meals)
```

Here is an example of how you can prompt the user to input a varying number of entries. If, however you mess up the conditional expression you can leave the user frustratedly inputting in an infinite loop.

This infinite loop is a gracious one, it doesn't overload your processor, since the program stops after each iteration and waits for users input. If, however, you wouldn't wait for user input and execute heavy computation tasks (like loading files, searching through big lists, etc.), the python process would quickly overload itself and potentially freeze.

```
meals = []
userInput = input("Enter a meal you enjoy(done to quit)\n")
while userInput == userInput:
    meals.append(userInput)
    userInput = input("Enter a meal you enjoy(done to quit)\n")
print(meals)
```

This infinite loop is a gracious one, it doesn't overload your processor, since the program stops after each iteration and waits for users input. If, however, you wouldn't wait for user input and execute heavy computation tasks (like loading files, searching through big lists, etc.), the python process would quickly overload itself and potentially freeze. Try this two-liner:

```
while True:
    print(2)
```

PROGRAMMING FUNCTIONS

INTRODUCTION

A function is a reusable block of code that encapsulates a single related action. The purpose behind this is to organize the code into modules each of which handles a specific part of the overall programs' logic so it can be easily reused, improved and managed.

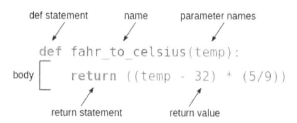

In this introduction, we have already used various different built-in functions, now we are finally ready to create some of our own. All functions begin with the keyword '**def**' followed by the function name and parentheses, ending with a colon to indicate the code block for the function – similarly to conditional expressions and loops.

```
def myFunction():
    print("Hi, I'm the function you were looking for!")

for x in range(10):
    myFunction()
```

In this simple example, we have a function that just prints out some text and we call it just like we called the built-in functions, but this time from a loop – which results in the function being called 10 times. Now this is not a very sensible function since we can just type in the print statement inside the for loop and not bother with functions at all, so let us correct this mistake and move forward with a better example.

```
def compute100sum():
    sum = 0
    for x in range(101):
        sum = sum + x
    print(sum)

userIn = input("Would you like to compute the sum of the first 100 numbers? y/n\n")
if userIn == 'y':
    compute100sum()
else:
    userIn = input("Last chance to compute the sum, do you want to? y/n\n")
    if userIn == 'y':
        compute100sum()
        print("You almost missed out on a great opportunity")
    else:
        print("I guess you will never know")
```

In this example as you can see, we call the function at two different points in the program. We could still just write the code instead of the function name at the two points where we called it, however I encourage you to try and do it, so you can see for yourself how much messier the code gets, and this is only a small introductory example.

Imagine a function, long hundreds of rows, being called from 10 different places. Now replacing that function call with its' contents would be a real disaster. It would also be very redundant – as you would have 10 times the exact same code inside your source code.

By outsourcing these repeating code lines into function, you

- reduce the file size,
- remove redundancy and
- enhance the readability and maintainability of the code.

The use of functions to create **modularity** in your programs is not strictly a technical skill – it is more of a design skill, since you are not changing the overall performance of your code, but some of its meta-characteristics like readability, reusability, scalability etc.

If this seems somewhat pointless and/or subjective, worry not, as it becomes more and more useful the further down the coding journey you go. As projects get more complex and your programming intuition gets stronger you are going to start to incorporate functions intuitively into your code.

For now, when writing a program, remember to ask yourself – will these statements always come together, and will I need them **more than once** in my code? If the answer is yes, you should consider outsourcing them into a function.

PARAMETERS OF A FUNCTION

We already have some practical experience with function parameters, for instance every time we did user inputs, we specified a message to the user passed as a parameter to the 'input' function. We also passed parameters to the 'range' function, passed objects to the 'type' function etc.

Parameters are an important feature, because they allow us to create more responsive functions, because having parameters allows our function to change its' behavior based upon the parameters given. Here is the following scenario – we want to make a quiz program so we can compete with our friends.

```
def askQuestions(myDictionary, challenger):
    print(challenger," do your best to answer the following questions:\n")
    count = 0
    for question in myDictionary:
        ans = input(question)
        if ans == myDictionary[question]:
            count = count + 1
            print("Correct answer!\n")
        else:
            print("Wrong answer!\n")
    print(challenger," you got ",count," questions correct!\n")

myDict = {
    '2 + 2 = ?\n':'4',
    '3 * 3 = ?\n':'9',
    'What is the capitol of Germany?\n':'Berlin',
    "What's the integral of x^2 over 0 to 1?\n":'1'
}

contestants = input('Please enter the names of the contestants separated with a
space:\n').split()

for cont in contestants:
    askQuestions(myDict,cont)
```

Hopefully, it becomes evident how using a function in this scenario makes the code much more readable and easier to use/change. Obviously, we can just copy the initialization and the loop through the contestants in the askQuestions function to achieve the same result, however take a moment to appreciate how intuitively the logical flow of the program is. We initialize the questions and ask the user to enter the contestants, after which, each contestant gets quizzed and his score displayed.

The **askQuestions** function does exactly what it says – it asks you the questions. After some time, I might decide I want to add a different function that asks selects a subset of questions from a larger set, I might decide I want to give each player an overall score and give stronger players, harder questions etc. Eventually the program can become quite complex, at which point it is really useful for you as a programmer to be able to know what a function does what without having to read all of the code inside the function.

I can see that the function takes in a question set and a challenger name and implements all of the question-asking functionality inside, therefore if I want to make a change to the way the questions are asked, I know I need to modify this function, if I need to do something else, I can rely on this function doing exactly what it says and not worry that it might have some unforeseen impact on the code I am worrying about.

RETURN VALUE OF A FUNCTION

We talked about what a function is, how we can alter a functions' behavior by using parameters, it is only logical to consider the final piece of the puzzle – that is how can functions give us feedback. You guessed it! We do that by using the return statement.

Imagine the following scenario – our friend group is nerdy and somewhat forgetful and thus when we get together to play DnD we often forget our dies. Since you are an awesome programmer you decide to create a backup next time this happens.

```python
from random import randrange

def ThrowDie(character, numberOfSides):
    if numberOfSides == 20:
        return randrange(20)+1
    elif numberOfSides == 6:
        return randrange(6)+1
    elif numberOfSides == 4:
        return randrange(4)+1
    else:
        print("Such a die does not exist!")

FrodosDie = ThrowDie('Frodo', 6)
print('Frodo threw a ', FrodosDie)
```

Not only functions can encapsulate certain functionality, but they can communicate the result of the functionality with other parts of the code. If we decide that we want to expand our program I can just use the ThrowDie function inside another function that calculates the amount of damage our character is going to inflict, for example.

If you consider our previous example with the quizzing program – now that we know what return statements do, we can opt to return the score of each player and save it to create a leaderboard or to create some other functionality.

DOCSTRINGS

Going back to our discussion about functions serving as a design tool – Docstrings facilitate this further, by allowing us to document the behavior of our functions in a way that can be itself – functionally invoked.

Allow me to explain. Obviously, it is a good idea to give descriptions of your functions so whoever reads them or needs to edit them later can figure what were you trying to do with this code. Docstrings are a little bit more different than simple comments, because there is a method that allows programs to read the documentation of certain functions – the docstring is that documentation.

```
def square(x):
    '''square function takes in a single argument and returns its square '''
    return x ** 2

print(square.__doc__)
```

So docstrings are created by using triple quotes or triple double-quotes, and can be invoked by using the '__doc__' method, you might be wondering what those fancy underscores are, but worry not, we are going to cover that in the upcoming Object-Oriented Programming chapter.

Code is written once, but it is read and edited many times, this is why detailed explanations of functions are a key skill that any esteemed programmer should have. Even the creators of Python decided that it would be for the best if their code is well documented so, you can try and call the __doc__ method on all the built-in functions that you would like.

```
print(print.__doc__)
```

TYPE CHECKING

As we discussed in the first chapter – unlike most languages, Python is a dynamically typed language and it does not require the programmer to specify the type of the variable he is using. Not only that, but a variable can change it's type during the execution of the program, which may introduce issues when handling the variable.

```
def greeter_func(name: str) -> None:
    print("Hi,",name)

greeter_func("George")
```

The way this function works would be exactly the same if we did not use type checking, that is to say – type checking falls in a similar category to docstrings in that it provides us with a more readable code, which makes it less likely that the programmer will make wrong assumptions, about some variable or function in the code.

In the example we define a function that takes in a single parameter – our name and just prints it out. 'name' is our function parameter and colon 'str' indicates that we are expecting 'name' to be of type 'str'. Similarly, the arrow followed by 'None' is the syntax for type checking the return value of our function, so in this example what we are telling Python is that we are expecting the function to not have a return value. Let us do another example.

```
def addIntegers(x: int, y: int) -> int:
    return x+y

print(addIntegers("I'm feeling"," mischeavous"))
```

You will notice that even though I specified that 'x' and 'y' should be integers and that the return value should be also an integer – neither of those are actually true. Which highlights the fact that type checking serves a design purpose.

If you want to you can violate the types, but then you will be faced with the possibility of your code producing unforeseen results, but you wont be prevented from doing so. In this case we are clearly stating that we would like to add together integers, however when we pass in two strings – what actually happens is we concatenate them.

Note that we can actually make Python 'enforce' typings – that is throw an error for every violated type, thus allowing only programs that have successfully passed type-checking to be executed, this however will be discussed at a later chapter, when we get into the subject of Python scripts.

RECURSIVE FUNCTIONS

Remember how I told you how functions are more of a design thing – well I lied. That is mostly true, with the exception of recursive functions.

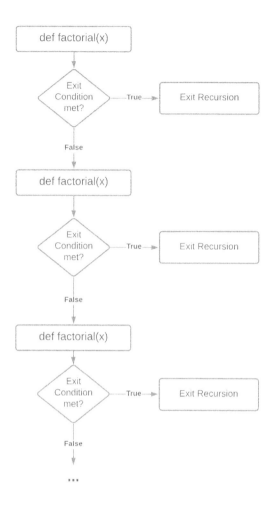

A recursive function is a function that calls itself. That might sound crazy, since a deterministic function should always produce the same results, so wouldn't having a function call itself result in an infinite loop? Well, you are almost correct, remember when we talked about parameters and how they can modify the behavior of the function? Yeah, that is how we will force the function to end.

Just like with while loops we run the danger of running into infinite loops, as there is always the possibility for a function to call itself for eternity. This is why the first thing you must consider is the base case – what is the condition upon which a function will stop calling itself. Here is an example – we want to calculate the factorial of a number – the product of all positive numbers leading up to it. If you are still not sure what it is, remember that the top skill of a programmer is – being able to find the correct answers on the internet.

```
def factorial(x):
    '''
    Takes in a single argument x and returns
    it\'s factorial,
    which is the product of
    all numbers from 1 to X
    '''
    if x == 1:
        return 1
    else:
        return factorial(x-1)*x

x = int(input("Enter a number less than 10\n"))
print("The factorial of", x, "is",factorial(x))
```

Let us first think about the logical flow of the function. The entire function is a conditional expression, therefore there are two possibilities, one of which is to call the function again (but with a different parameter) and the other is to return the fixed value of 1.

Notice that each time the function does a recursive call – the value of the parameter is reduced by one. If for instance you were to call the function with a negative initial parameter it would just keep on decreasing until a stack overflow is reached, because the base case will never be reached.

Let us assume that that is not the case, or better yet – modify the base case to be lesser-than-or-equal to one so there are no gaping holes in our logic. Following this example – calling factorial(5) will result in 5 recursive calls to the factorial function. The base case is factorial(1) and that is what guarantees our function will end successfully. It is worth noting that even though it looks similar to a loop where we iterate through each and every element, there is a very important distinction. Namely – our first call to the function returns 5*f(4) which is not a value.

What actually happens is we go down the recursion and once we reach the base case, we start going back up substituting the function call for the value we already know. f(1) is substituted for 1, then f(2) is substituted for 2, f(3) is substituted for 6, f(4) is substituted for 24 and finally, since we now know that f(4) = 24, we can calculate that f(5) = 5*f(4) is equal to 120.

This may seem like a pointless example, because you can achieve the same thing with a simple for loop and you are correct, however the aim of the example is to illustrate the concept of recursion as it is considered a more advanced topic. Later down the road when you start learning about graph and tree structures and how to traverse them, recursion will become an indispensable tool.

OBJECT-ORIENTED PROGRAMMING

INTRODUCTION

We spent most of the course using built-in objects and we even mentioned that everything in python is an object, but we dodged the question – what an object actually is. Now we are finally going to address it and combine all that we learned from previous chapters in a cohesive way into objects.

Object-Oriented Programming (OOP) is a method by which we bundle together related properties and actions in individual objects.

Consider we want to model a car in Python, we would like to have a name variable, a measure of how full is the gas tank and we would like to be able to drive a car. All of these things are inter-related so, just like with functions – it makes sense to couple them together from a design perspective.

CLASSES AND INSTANCES

THE BASIS FOR OOP ARE CLASSES AND INSTANCES.

A class is the blueprint of an object, while the instance is the object itself.

The blueprint is the house class – as it specifies what a house is – something having a roof, walls, a door etc. Notice how the class does not specify exactly what is a house – it only tells us what a house has. House instances however are specific manifestations of a house. They all conform to the class, by having all the specified properties, but each house can be different to the next – one can have a red roof, while the other can have a blue roof.

```
class House:
    def __init__(self,roofColor,wallColor,doorDesign):

        self.roofColor = roofColor
        self.wallColor = wallColor
        self.doorDesign = doorDesign

weirdHouse = House('Blue','Gray','Classic')
fancyHouse = House('Red','Gray','Modern')

print(fancyHouse.roofColor)
```

Let me just mention that functions within classes are called methods/class methods/object methods etc.

Now let us unpack this. The class is initialized by using the 'class' keyword following with the class name. Inside the scope of the class, the first thing we see is this strange method with double underscores. Just like with the __doc__ method it is something inherent for Python and is used to initialize a class.

'self' is also a Python specific keyword – it is a reference to the instance of the class that is being invoked. So, when we say self.roofColor = 'Red', what we are telling Python is – I want the instance of the class being referred to, to have the property 'roofColor' be set to 'Red'. Back to the example, what we are telling Python is, that in order to create a 'House' object we need to pass in 3 parameters each of which will be a specific property of the object.

The objects in this case are 'weirdHouse' and 'fancyHouse' and both of them have slightly different properties. We can easily check that, by using the (dot) operator. Put in words, what it stands for is – Access this specific variable/method of this specific object.

Let us do another example.

```
class Car:
    def __init__(self, brand, model, percentFuel, yearProduced):
        self.brand = brand
        self.model = model
        self.percentFuel = percentFuel
        self.yearProduced = yearProduced

myVW = Car('VW','Beetle',0.3,2010)
myMazda = Car('Mazda','323',1.0,2003)
```

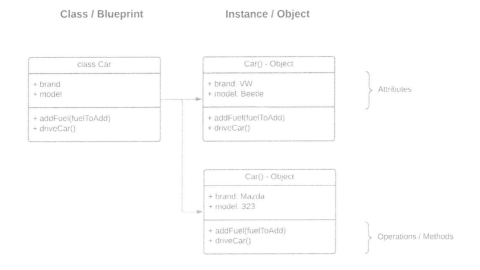

Just as before, we create the class by using the class keyword, then in the class body – we immediately define the __init__ function, so we can initialize our object variables. Outside of the function we create two instances of the class with those specific variables set to them.

CLASS METHODS

So far, we created classes that hold variables, now we will extend that courtesy to functions, except – when they are in classes, we will call them methods.

```python
class Car:
    def __init__(self, brand, model, percentFuel, yearProduced):
        self.brand = brand
        self.model = model
        self.percentFuel = percentFuel
        self.yearProduced = yearProduced

    def addFuel(self, fuelToAdd):
        if fuelToAdd + self.percentFuel > 1:
            print("Warning danger of petrol spill!")
            self.percentFuel = 1
        else:
            self.percentFuel = self.percentFuel + fuelToAdd

    def driveCar(self):
        if self.percentFuel > 0.1:
            print("Brrrrrrm..")
            self.percentFuel = self.percentFuel - 0.1
        else:
            print("The",self.brand,self.model,"fails to start")

myVW = Car('VW','Beetle',1,2010)

myMazda = Car('Mazda','323',0,2003)

myVW.addFuel(1)

myMazda.driveCar()
myMazda.addFuel(0.5)
myMazda.driveCar()
```

Now we have added some functionality to our Car object. We can drive our car and we can add fuel to it. The logic of the methods is pretty straightforward, so I am not going to go into detail about it. However, I will turn your attention to two facts – for every class method, the first parameter should always be self, this tells Python that what we are dealing with variables of the instance that called that specific method. For the same reason we call every object variable prefixed with self.

DUNDER METHODS

Dunder is a contraction of **D**ouble **under**score, sometimes also called magic methods. So far, we have used the __init__ method and the __doc__ method. There is however a large quantity of Dunder methods, so for the purposes of this introduction we are only going to look at a few.

When working with the default object types like int, string, float, etc. We have a lot of our functionality implemented for us. For instance, it is fairly obvious how adding two numbers works, however when we create our own class - 'Car' and we decide on adding two instances of it - Volkswagen and a Mazda it is not very clear cut what that should do – that is why it is left to the programmer to decide on the appropriate meaning for the respective operators, you might read about this exact same topic referred to by – operator overloading.

```python
class Order:
    def __init__(self,cart,orderId):
        self.cart = list(cart)
        self.orderId = orderId

    def __add__(self, other):
        self.cart.append(other)
        return self

myOrder = Order(['Orange','Pear','Banana'],101)
forgotToBuy = ['Pizza','Fries','Chocolates']

for item in forgotToBuy:
    myOrder = myOrder + item

print(myOrder.cart)
```

In this example we are creating a shopping cart class. To do so we initialize it as usual, using the __init__ method. In this case we also specify the __add__ method which overloads the functionality of the '+' operator. Since Python has no way of knowing what we mean when we say add this to our shopping cart object – this is the way for us to tell it. When we say add this to my shopping cart, it makes sense to put it in the cart, so that is exactly what we do, our shopping cart is a list and we define adding things to the cart to be equivalent to appending the item to the list.

Notice that we end the operator overloading with the statement 'return self' that is, because Python expects to receive an object of the same type with which we initially started. As expected, the items we add in the cart end up appended in that list.

```python
class Order:
    def __init__(self,cart,orderId):
        self.cart = list(cart)
        self.orderId = orderId

    def __add__(self, other):
        self.cart.append(other)
        return self

    def __getitem__(self,key):
        return self.cart[key]

myOrder = Order(['Orange','Pear','Banana'],101)
forgotToBuy = ['Pizza','Fries','Chocolates']

for item in forgotToBuy:
    myOrder = myOrder + item

for i in range(4):
    print(myOrder[i])
```

Another example of a Dunder method is the __getitem__ method – which tells us what does it mean when we try to retrieve a value by index from our object. In this case it makes the most sense to return the I-th item from the cart.

CLASS INHERITANCE

Another fundamental concept of OOP is inheritance. It is most intuitively described as an is-a relationship. For example, a house is-a type of building, in this case the building is the parent class and the house is the child class. That is because all houses are buildings, but not all buildings are houses.

Class Inheritance (or Parent-Child Relationships) are especially common in bigger projects and frameworks (like Django). So it's crucial you understand it and try the following examples on your machine.

Vehicle is a parent class, it specifies things common to all vehicles, they use some sort of fuel, are used for driving, etc. Whilst the child classes of vehicle are types of vehicle who share all of the properties of being a vehicle, but have other specific properties of theirs. For instance, a Bus vehicle has more than 10 seats and weights a lot more than cars or bikes and it requires a special driver's permit. Bikes on the other hand reach high top speeds, are very fuel efficient and have only two tires.

Let us do an example to help illustrate the concept. Our parent class will be 'Warrior' and our child classes would be 'Ninja' and 'Knight'.

```
class Warrior:
    def __init__(self,weapon,style,origin):
        self.weapon = weapon
        self.style = style
        self.origin = origin

    def attack(self):
        print("*Generic attacking noises*")

    def checkStatus(self):
        print("Warrior is ready to fight")

class Ninja(Warrior):
    def __init__(self):
        Warrior.__init__(self,'Katana','Agile','Japan')

    def attack(self):
        print("The katana nimbly slashes through the air")

    def specialAttack(self):
        print("Shuriken throw!")

class Knight(Warrior):
    def __init__(self):
        Warrior.__init__(self,['Broadsword','Shield'],'Endurance','Europe')

    def attack(self):
        print("With a confident swing, the broadsword cuts through the air ")

    def specialAttack(self):
        print("Shield bash!")

myWarrior = Warrior('Bow','Long-range','Steppes')
myNinja = Ninja()
myKnight = Knight()

myKnight.checkStatus()
myKnight.specialAttack()
myKnight.attack()
print()

myNinja.checkStatus()
myNinja.attack()
myNinja.specialAttack()

print()
myWarrior.checkStatus()
myWarrior.attack()
```

We start out in the same way, using the class specified followed by the class name, but when we define the child classes, we specify in parentheses who is the parent class that they inherit. What is the use of inheriting then? You will see that the Parent (Base) class has a function 'checkStatus' that is only implemented inside of it, however due to 'Ninja' and 'Warrior' being child classes of that class – they also can use that function.

Furthermore, 'attack' is implemented in the Base class, but each of the child classes have their own implementation of that method and when we call that method from the child classes, we get the result of their own function, not the generic one. This is what we call function overloading, as we have the same function multiple times. The function that will be called is the most specific function – the one that is in the child class.

There is also no problem with having specific method to each of the child classes, like in this example – with the 'specialAttack' method.

DJANGO 3

WHY DJANGO?

WEB FRAMEWORK

Let's find out what a web framework is. A web framework provides a set of tools that helps us in solving many of the common problems that occur in web development:

- URL routing

- accessing database

- manipulating data

- security,

- templates and much more.

Suppose you were to create a web application from scratch (in any programming language). In that case, you will face the problems just mentioned and would have to solve them yourself – a very long journey. A framework can help solve these problems out of the box so you can focus on getting actual work done.

> *We use a web framework (or any programming framework for that matter) not to reinvent the wheel.*

POPULARITY OF DJANGO

Why Django? Because it is one of the best web frameworks Python has to offer. It has an active community and countless modules on the python package library. It means, if you are facing a problem, someone else has likely solved it, and you can utilize their modules to speed up your development.

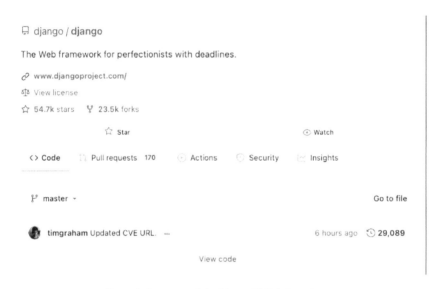

Figure 1 - Summary of the Django GitHub Repository

With 24k forks (as of the beginning of 2021), the Django Web Framework surpasses Laravel (a PHP Web Framework with 20k forks) and Ruby on Rails (Ruby Web Framework with 19k forks). This tells you that the users and community behind Django are gigantic. This, in turn, tells you, as already mentioned, that a lot of the tasks that you want to solve probably already have been solved.

It is used by big corporations like Instagram, Disqus, Youtube, and many more. Django was built with the idea of developing web applications as fast as possible. It provides many useful features out of the box, such as a ready-to-use authentication system, flash messages, password reset, and much more.

MODEL-VIEW-CONTROLLER PATTERN

Model-View-Controller (MVC) is a design pattern in which we separate the logic, data, and the UI into separate layers. It is a fancy way to say that we have dissembled our Python Code in different *files* depending on what the code does.

MODEL

This is the place where all of your data gets directly managed. Think of it as a blueprint for your data – but expressed in Code. With data usually being stored in a database.

Inside a Model you we tell your Application how to perform basic CRUD Operations on our data. (Reminder! CRUD = Create; Read; Update; Delete). The Model Layern then performs the final operations on the data in a Database.

VIEW

This part of the pattern deals with displaying content and data to the user. HTML, CSS, Javascript & Static Assets are defined here. For example, a productTemplate.html would belong to the View Layer.

CONTROLLER

The controller is the middleman between View and the Model. A Controller takes data from the model (which in turn speaks to the database), processes the data and passes it to the view.

Now the following will be slightly confusing: Django uses a design pattern that is very similar to the MVC - **Model-View-Template** (MVT). In simple terms,

- The **Model** in MVT is the same as the MVC's Model.
- The **View** in MVT acts as the Controller (business logic) in the application.
- The **Template** in MVT is the same as the MVC's Template.

The following Figure compares the MVC and MVT while also highlighting the purposes of each Layer and the flow of Data.

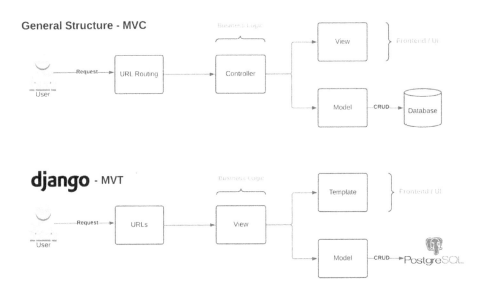

ENVIRONMENT SETUP

We will be using only three resources that are free and partially open source. Python 3.8+ being the most important one. While the Database is secondary since you can choose another backend for your Django Application – meaning you can choose to store your data in an **SQLite** file or another Database.

- Python 3.8+

- PostgreSQL Database Server

- pgAdmin 4 (GUI for the DB Server)

POSTGRESQL ON WINDOWS

We will be using PostgreSQL as our database for this project. To install PostgreSQL, head over to https://www.enterprisedb.com/downloads/postgres-postgresql-downloads, and download PostgreSQL for your OS. Since I'm using 64-bit Windows, I chose the "Windows x86-64" setup for the latest version, which at the time of writing is 13.1.

Figure 2 - Download Page for PostgreSQL Server

The setup process is pretty straightforward. You'll be prompted to select an installation directory. I'm installing it in a directory called "POSTGRESQL" on my C drive.

In the following step, you can select different components to install. We need the components PostgreSQL Server, pgAdmin 4, and Command Line Tools. We don't need the Stack builder. In the next step, leave the data directory to default, a directory called "data." You will be asked to set a password for the admin user of the database. Please remember the password, as we will need it later to connect to our database. For local development, a "12345" will be enough.

Figure 3 - It's crucial to remember this password

Next, select a port for the database. Setting it to default "5432" is recommended. The final step should be left to default also. If you're on a Mac, the steps described above are similar, and you have to leave everything to default. Just don't install Stack

Builder that comes bundled with this setup. Install the pgAdmin4 and everything else. Again, remember your password!

If this setup worked fine for you, skip the next section. If you run into some troubles, give it a try with docker in the following chapter.

POSTGRESQL ON LINUX (WITH DOCKER)

It's recommended to use Docker for several reasons. One of them is that your host machine doesn't get trashed with different Services and Service versions. Think of docker **for** PostgreSQL as *virtualenv* is **for** python packages. If your next Django Project requires an older version of PostgreSQL, you can easily manage that with docker.

Assuming that you have docker installed, we'll briefly touch upon PostgreSQL with Docker. First, pull the latest image.

Terminal

```
root@internetuser:/home/internetuser# docker pull postgres

Using default tag: latest

latest: Pulling from library/postgres
```

Now that we have pulled the latest Postgres Image let's verify it.

```
root@internetuser:/home/internetuser# docker images

REPOSITORY       TAG              IMAGE ID         CREATED         SIZE

postgres         latest           a6cd86e1dfce     11 days ago     314MB
```

We need to launch the Image in a Container that will open ports 5432 to access the database from our local machine. Set the name of the Container to whatever you want.

```
root@internetuser:/home/internetuser# docker run --name finance_blog_db -e
POSTGRES_PASSWORD=finblogPW -d -p 5432:5432 postgres

13b79ceceeebef0e33dedeffe5cb83f780f7f168cb74cd3a084ab634448c2599

root@internetuser:/home/internetuser# docker container ls

CONTAINER ID     IMAGE            COMMAND              CREATED
        STATUS              PORTS                   NAMES

13b79ceceeeb     postgres         "docker-entrypoint.s…"   7 seconds ago        Up 6
seconds          0.0.0.0:5432->5432/tcp    finance_blog_db
```

The option "-e" specifies the Environment Variable "**POSTGRES_PASSWORD**" inside the Container. Postgres will create an Admin user with the username "**postgres**" and the supplied password. You must use these credentials to log in to the database in PGAdmin4.

> IMPORTANT NOTE: THIS DOCKER CONTAINER IS SAVING ALL THE DATA INSIDE ITSELF. WHICH MEANS THE DATA WILL BE LOST WHEN THE CONTAINER FAILS OR YOUR HOST SYSTEM RESTARTS. WHILE NOT IDEAL FOR PRODUCTION, IT'S IDEAL FOR OUR PURPOSE OF LEARNING ABOUT DJANGO, SINCE YOU CAN FLUSH THE

DATABASE BY RESTARTING THE CONTAINER.

BASICS

PROJECTS VS. APPLICATION

THEORY

You will see the terms "project" and "application" repeatedly in this book, so we need to clarify the difference between them. Long story short:

- project = project (e.g., netflix.com, youtube.com)
- application = service (e.g., blog.netflix.com, stream.netflix.com, billing.netflix.com, etc.)

PROJECT

A project is a complete Django Application with settings, media, templates, configurations, etc. A project is the most significant unit in terms of file structures. You can zip a Django project folder, and it will contain every source code and functionality that your Application has. The data won't be included as it resides in the Database.

Django projects must have one or more application(s) – which is the next smaller unit in our Application representation. For example, your Web Application is a project. It will have different functionalities (applications) like blogposts, user authentication, comment section, portfolio management, etc.

APPLICATION

Inside a project, you typically have a couple of applications. Each application has one or many functionalities, and they may be reused in other projects as well.

A Django Application is a group of

- Views – think code with business logic

- Models – think code that describes your data

- Templates – think HTML Layouts that your users interact with

- URLs – think URL-router for your Django Website

An empty Application (boilerplate) in Django has the following folder structure. We'll take a closer look at each file in the following chapters.

Terminal

```
$: ls application_name/
total 40
-rw-r--r--  1 a.bulezyuk  0B   __init__.py
-rw-r--r--  1 a.bulezyuk  63B  admin.py
-rw-r--r--  1 a.bulezyuk  83B  apps.py
drwxr-xr-x  3 a.bulezyuk  96B  migrations
-rw-r--r--  1 a.bulezyuk  57B  models.py
-rw-r--r--  1 a.bulezyuk  60B  tests.py
-rw-r--r--  1 a.bulezyuk  63B  views.py
```

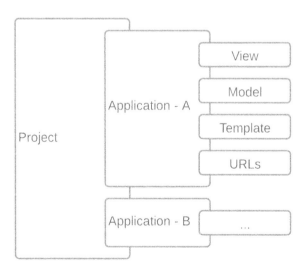

Before we take a closer look at the files in the terminal, let's set up your development environment and create a boilerplate Django Application on your local machine.

PRACTICE

VIRTUAL ENVIRONMENT

It is preferred to use a virtual environment to isolate our Python 3 projects to use different versions of the same package for different projects. By default, you can only have one version of a package installed at a time in a Python environment.

We'll make use of **virtualenv** – but feel free to explore **pipenv** and **pyenv**. Create a directory called "MyProject" and cd into it. Open your command prompt or terminal and run the following to install virtual env:

Terminal

```
E:\MyProject> pip install virtualenv

E:\MyProject> virtualenv .
```

This command will create two directories in **MyProject**, Lib, and Scripts. Any packages you install in the virtualenv will now be saved to the **site-packages** directory found inside the Lib folder. Before we install anything, let's activate the virtual env.

Change directory into the newly created **Scripts** directory and type the following command to activate the virtual environment:

Terminal

```
E:\MyProject> cd Scripts

E:\MyProject\Scripts> activate

(MyProject) E:\MyProject\Scripts>
```

If you successfully activated the virtual environment, you should see the name of the root directory **(MyProject)** before the path in the command line or terminal. Success! From now on, every python library we install will be available only in this virtual environment and only when you successfully activate it.

Many of us face a common issue when we open a new terminal and forget to activate the current virtual environment. You end up with many Errors telling you that you are missing many python packages.

INSTALLING DJANGO

Now cd back to the root directory "MyProject" and install Django 3.

Terminal

```
(MyProject) E:\MyProject> pip install django
```

At the time of making this, I installed the latest Django version, which was 3.1.3. Once you have Django installed, run the following command to create a Django project:

Terminal

```
(MyProject) E:\MyProject> django-admin startproject financeblog
```

You will now have a new directory called **financeblog,** and it should have the following tree directory.

```
∨ financeblog
  ∨ financeblog
    🐍 __init__.py
    🐍 asgi.py
    🐍 settings.py
    🐍 urls.py
    🐍 wsgi.py
  🐍 manage.py
```

These files are:

- **manage.py** - A command-line utility through which you can interact with the Django project. We don't ever edit this file. As a Django developer, you use this file daily (at least for smaller projects).
- **finanaceblog/** - This directory is the core of your Django project with configuration files.

- **finanaceblog/__init__.py** - An empty file that tells Python to treat this file's directory as a package.
- **finanaceblog/asgi.py** - It is a configuration file for making our project run as an ASGI application.
- **finanaceblog/wsgi.py** - It is a configuration file for making our project run as a WSGI application.
- **finanaceblog/settings.py** - It includes all the settings required for our project.
- **finanaceblog/urls.py** - This file holds all of the URL patterns in the application, and each URL pattern is mapped to a View.

Now cd into the main "**finanaceblog**" project folder and run the following command to start the project:

Terminal

```
(MyProject) E:\MyProject\financeblog>python manage.py runserver
```

Doing so will start a development server. Django comes with a lightweight development server that automatically restarts every time it detects any changes to the project's source code. Note that this applies only to development. In production, we will have to set up a separate server. Running the above command will output the following information to the command prompt/terminal:

```
Watching for file changes with StatReloader
Performing system checks...


System check identified no issues (0 silenced).


You have 18 unapplied migration(s). Your project may not work properly until you
apply the migrations for app(s): admin, auth, contenttypes, sessions.
Run 'python manage.py migrate' to apply them.
Django version 3.1.3, using settings 'financeblog.settings'
Starting development server at http://127.0.0.1:8000/
Quit the server with CTRL-BREAK.
```

Now open your web browser and head over to http://127.0.0.1:8000/, and you will see the following screen

Figure 4 - Welcome Screen of a newly installed Django Project

That's it. With only a couple of Command-line executions and zero codings, we have launched a website. But…with no functionalities. And…with no Database connection. At least we now have a nice rocket.

DJANGO PROJECT SETTINGS

Before moving further, let's quickly look at the configurations in the "**settings.py**" file inside the project's "**financeblog**" directory. Django has many settings in this file, but we will take a look at the most important ones:

1. **BASE_DIR:** A *constant* that points to the root directory of your project.

2. **DEBUG:** This will be true by default. It tells Django that we are in development mode, and Django will show detailed error messages. This must be set to *False* when moving the website to production. Because we don't want to show random users our inner debug messages for security reasons.

3. **ALLOWED_HOSTS:** This is a list of domains that your Django site can serve. It needs to be configured in production when **DEBUG** is set to *False*.

4. **INSTALLED_APPS:** This includes a list of applications that have been enabled for this project. *Simply adding applications or plugins to a Django project does not enable them. You must include them in this list.*

5. **ROOT_URLCONF:** Points to a file where your root URL patterns are defined. We'll cover this file later.

When deploying to production, you'll use some sort of server. You will need to tell your WSGI Application where the settings file is located. You can do this by setting the environment variable DJANGO_SETTINGS_MODULE. In our case, you would insert something like '**financeblog.settings**'.

You can also use settings to set some global variables that every application needs access to. In the application, you can then check the value of a variable.

```
from django.conf import settings
if settings.DEBUG:
    # Do something
```

CONNECTING TO THE DATABASE

CONFIGURING POSTGRESQL

We now have a working Django project installed. If you noticed the terminal message, it says that we have 18 unapplied migrations. This message is telling us that we have some database changes that haven't been saved yet. By default, Django comes with an SQLite database configuration, but we will be using PostgreSQL. Let's configure our database first.

Open pgAdmin 4 that we previously installed. On your first time opening the pgAdmin Client, you should see a "Set Master Password" Popup.

Figure 5 - Setting a master password for the pgAdmin UI Access

You have to set a master password. It will be used to access the pgAdmin 4 application – it's not the Database password! After you set the master password, you'll be prompted to log in as the 'postgres' user when connecting to the server. Here you have to put the password you chose at the setup process – this is the Database password!

Now, try to access the initial Database. As you can see, we currently have a single database called "postgres". We have to create a new database for our project. We will choose the same name as our Django project, i.e., "financeblog". Right-click on the "Databases" and select **Create** > **Database**.

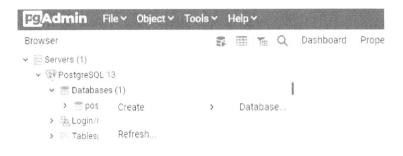

Figure 6 - Dropdown Menu to create a new Database in pgAdmin

Doing so will open a new window. Type "financeblog" in the field next to "Database" and hit the save button. This setup is entirely sufficient for learning purposes.

Figure 7 - UI Mask to create a new Database in pgAdmin

You will now have your database listed next to "postgres" database. It will not be activated and will have a red cross mark on it, as you can see. Right-click the "financeblog" database and select "connect database".

Figure 8 - Empty PostgreSQL Database for Django Project

That's it. Your database has been created and is up and running. It's still empty as we haven't created any tables yet.

CONFIGURING DJANGO CONNECTION

Now we have to connect our Django project to the database. By default, Django comes with a sqlite3 database configured – a Database that is stored as a file inside your project.

To use other databases, we have to configure the Django "**settings.py**". We will also need a python package called "**psycopg2**" which acts like a driver between python and PostgreSQL. Close the server on the command prompt and install psycopg2 via pip.

For Ubuntu Users: First, install libpq-dev by `sudo apt-get install libpq-dev`

Terminal

```
(MyProject) E:\MyProject\financeblog>pip install psycopg2
```

After installing the package, open the "**settings.py**" found inside your "**financeblog**" directory. Scroll down to the **DATABASES** setting.

```
DATABASES = {
    'default': {
        'ENGINE': 'django.db.backends.sqlite3',
        'NAME': BASE_DIR / 'db.sqlite3',
    }
}
```

Code 1 financeblog\financeblog\settings.py

Here we have to make some changes. Edit "**DATABASES**" dictionary like.

```
DATABASES = {
    'default': {
        'ENGINE': 'django.db.backends.postgresql_psycopg2',
        'NAME': 'financeblog',
        'USER': 'postgres',
        'PASSWORD': '12345',
        'HOST': '127.0.0.1',
        'PORT': '5432',
    }
}
```

Code 2 financeblog\financeblog\settings.py

1. **ENGINE:** We are telling Django to use PostgreSQL engine. It will use psycopg2 for this. The value is the path to the package/engine.

2. **NAME:** The name of the database we created.

3. **USER:** Name of the database user we will use to access the database. It's Postgres.

4. **PASSWORD:** Password of the user postgres. I chose mine to be 12345 at install time. You have to put your password here.

5. **HOST:** This tells Django the location of our database. It is localhost.

6. **PORT:** This tells Django the port at which our database listens. The default would be 5432 unless you changed it.

Django comes with a couple of built-in database backend.

Table 1: Built-in Database Engines

Database	Django Engine Path
PostgreSQL	django.db.backends.postgresql
MySQL	django.db.backends.mysql
SQlite	django.db.backends.sqlite3
Oracle	django.db.backends.oracle

DJANGO DATABASE MIGRATION

WHAT IS MIGRATION?

Migration is a way of propagating changes made to data structure (saved in models.py) into your database schema. Think of migration as git for the database schema.

In Django, you declare your Data Models (**models** = think SQL **Tables**) in *models.py*. In *models.py,* you also define their attributes (model **attributes** = think **Columns** of a SQL Table).

Your Data Models will grow and change over time – you add a column A, you change the maximum length of column B, and you delete column C. Each time you perform these changes in your *model.py*, you have to propagate these changes to the Database (PostgreSQL in our case) – Django migrations are here to do this task.

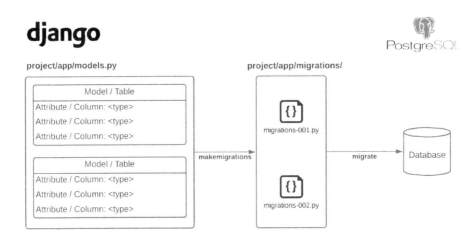

Figure 9 - Translation of Data Model in models.py into actual DB Changes

Django 3 for Beginners

The workflow of a Django migration is rather simple, as shown in the Figure before:

1.   Create Migration(s)
2.   Apply Migration(s)

CREATE MIGRATIONS

To package up your model.py changes into migration files (**migration file** = think **git commit**) use the ***makemigration*** command. This command will generate the mentioned migration files. The migration files for each Application will be saved in the "**migrations**" directory inside that Application directory.

Terminal

```
(My Project): python manage.py makemigrations
```

APPLY MIGRATIONS

When you create a new Django Project, the initial migrations are already made for you. That's why we can omit the previously mentioned **makemigrations** command. We proceed with the second command in the workflow - **migrate**. This command will read the previously generated migration files, translate them into SQL and update the Database Schema.

```
(MyProject) E:\MyProject\financeblog>python manage.py migrate
```

```
Operations to perform:
  Apply all migrations: admin, auth, contenttypes, sessions
Running migrations:
  Applying contenttypes.0001_initial... OK
  Applying auth.0001_initial... OK
  Applying admin.0001_initial... OK
  Applying admin.0002_logentry_remove_auto_add... OK
  Applying admin.0003_logentry_add_action_flag_choices... OK
  Applying contenttypes.0002_remove_content_type_name... OK
  Applying auth.0002_alter_permission_name_max_length... OK
  Applying auth.0003_alter_user_email_max_length... OK
  Applying auth.0004_alter_user_username_opts... OK
  Applying auth.0005_alter_user_last_login_null... OK
  Applying auth.0006_require_contenttypes_0002... OK
  Applying auth.0007_alter_validators_add_error_messages... OK
  Applying auth.0008_alter_user_username_max_length... OK
  Applying auth.0009_alter_user_last_name_max_length... OK
  Applying auth.0010_alter_group_name_max_length... OK
  Applying auth.0011_update_proxy_permissions... OK
  Applying auth.0012_alter_user_first_name_max_length... OK
  Applying sessions.0001_initial... OK
```

Now head back to pgAdmin and open **financeblog>Schemas>public>Tables**.

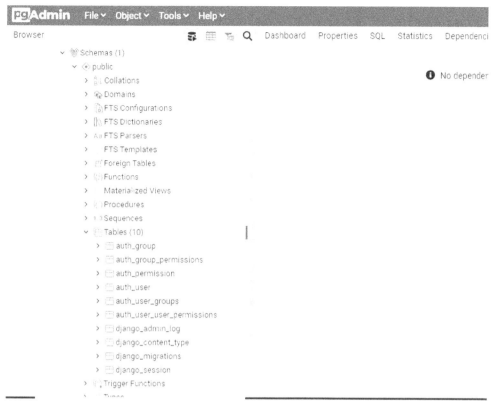

Figure 10 - Django 3 Core Tables saved in PostgreSQL Database.

You can see now that our **financeblog** database has 10 tables. This means our Django database connection configuration was successful. Now rerun the dev server. You shouldn't see the "unapplied migrations'' message anymore – that message was displayed at the first start of the dev server.

Terminal

```
(MyProject) E:\MyProject\financeblog>python manage.py runserver
Watching for file changes with StatReloader
Performing system checks...

System check identified no issues (0 silenced).
Django version 3.1.3, using settings 'financeblog.settings'
Starting development server at http://127.0.0.1:8000/
Quit the server with CTRL-BREAK.
```

CREATING A NEW APPLICATION

MANAGE.PY STARTAPP

Let's create our first Django Application. Remember, an Application in Django is similar to service for your websites like a blog service, a billing service or a booking service. Django provides a command utility that builds the boilerplate structure for us. Go to the root directory of your project and run the following command to create an app called "blog".

Terminal

```
(MyProject) E:\MyProject\financeblog>python manage.py startapp blog
```

This command will bootstrap a new App inside our Django Project. The CLI (Comman Line Interface) will create pre-populated python files inside that folder. Pretty handy.

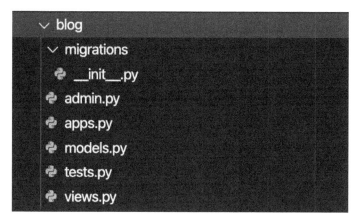

Figure 11 - Folder Structure of a newly created Django 3 Application

1. **admin.py:** You include your models in this file if you want to show them on Django's administration site. We'll cover it in the following sections. Using this file is optional.
2. **apps.py:** We can configure our app's behaviour in this file.
3. **models.py:** We define our application's data models here. This file is required, but we can leave it blank if we aren't doing anything related to databases.
4. **tests.py:** Here, Django will look for tests for the current app.
5. **views.py:** This is the file where you write your business/application logic. Each view works with an HTTP request as its parameter and returns some sort of response.
6. **migrations/:** This folder will include any database migrations we create. That's the folder we talked about in the previous sections.

Whenever we create a new application in a Django project, we have to explicitly tell Django that we will be using this application. To do so, open the "**settings.py**" file in the "**financeblog**" directory and scroll down to this section:

```
INSTALLED_APPS = [
    'django.contrib.admin',
    'django.contrib.auth',
    'django.contrib.contenttypes',
    'django.contrib.sessions',
    'django.contrib.messages',
    'django.contrib.staticfiles',
]
```

Code 3 financeblog\financeblog\settings.py

In this list, add our newly created application like so:

```
INSTALLED_APPS = [
    'django.contrib.admin',
    'django.contrib.auth',
    'django.contrib.contenttypes',
    'django.contrib.sessions',
    'django.contrib.messages',
    'django.contrib.staticfiles',
    'blog'
]
```

Code 4 financeblog\financeblog\settings.py

DESIGNING THE BLOG SCHEMA

DEFINING THE ATTRIBUTES

We use models (from "Data Model") to define schemas. In Django, we create our models inside the "**models.py**" file of every application. A Django model is a python class that inherits from "**django.db.models.Model**".

Django will create a table in the Database for each model found inside our models file. The attributes of our model class will represent the columns inside the database table. With the class attributes, we specify the type of data a column will have.

Let's define a "**Blog**" data model by creating a Python Class with the name "Blog". Open the *models.py* file of our *blog* application and add the following code.

```python
from django.db import models
from django.utils import timezone
from django.contrib.auth.models import User
from django.urls import reverse
from django.core.validators import MinLengthValidator

content_validator = MinLengthValidator(limit_value=300, message="Content should be at leas
t 300 characters long!")

class Blog(models.Model):
    title = models.CharField(max_length=250)
    content = models.TextField(validators=[content_validator])
    date_published = models.DateTimeField(default=timezone.now)
    author = models.ForeignKey(User, on_delete=models.CASCADE)

    def __str__(self):
        return self.title

    def get_absolute_url(self):
        return reverse("blog_detail", kwargs={'pk': self.pk})
```

Code 5 financeblog\blog\models.py

Let's take a look at the attributes we just wrote inside the "**Blog**" model. Remember, these class attributes will create columns in the PostgreSQL Table "blog" when we make the migrations.

1. **title**: This field is for our blog title. It is a *CharField* that will become a *VARCHAR* column inside our database.
2. **content:** This is the body of the blog. It is a *TextField* that will become a *TEXT* column in our database.
3. **date_published:** It is a DateTime value that indicates when the post was created. We are setting the option **auto_now_add** to *True*, which indicates that it will automatically set the current date whenever an object is created.
4. **author:** A *ForeignKey* field in Django means a **Many-To-One** field. It will define a many-to-one relationship between a blog object/row and a user object/row. It means a user creates a blog, and a user can create many blogs. In our database, the *primary key* (primary key = **pk**; think **id**) of the related User will be saved to this field. The **on_delete=models.CASCADE** option means that if the associated User is deleted, we want to delete this blog.

Note that we didn't create this User model. Django gives us an authentication system out of the box, which has a User model. We are importing the User model in the third line.

The __str__ method is used to create a human-readable version of the object. We are returning the title of the blog. Whenever we print an instance of the blog or view it on the admin site (discussed in the following sections), Django will display the blog title instead of something unreadable (like the Python Object itself).

Following is an overview of other field Types that Django provides us with. You can use any of these field types from the table by creating instances of the mentioned classes like:

```
field_name = models.<field-type>(parameters)
```

Some of them will be used later in this book. A full list of the available Fields was not shown since the list will grow and change with new versions. The most crucial aspect of this section is to understand that you define the fields in a model Class and have parameters and options.

Field Class	Description and Parameters
JSONField	New in Django 3.1. A Field for saving JSON Payloads. Incredibly convenient when working with REST APIs. Parameters: - encoder: simple JSON Class to serialize data - decoder: simple JSON Class to deserialize a value fetched from DB Example: ``` data = models.JSONField(null=True) ```
FileField	Parameters: - upload_to: Path in your project to the upload directory - storage: A Storage object that handles the retrieval and storage of your files Example: ``` attachment_one = models.FileField(upload_to='uploads/') ```
ImageField	Similar to FileField but with a Validator to ensure the File is an Image. Example: ``` models.ImageField(default="default.jpg", upload_to="profile_pictures") ```
EmailField	EmailField is basically a CharField with an EmailValidator Example: ``` Email = models.EmailField(max_length=50) ```

APPLYING MIGRATIONS

Remember, our Blog model represents a table in the database. The attributes of the model represent columns in the database table. Django doesn't automatically create the tables for our models. We have to tell Django to do that explicitly. There are two steps involved to push our model's schema to reflect on the database.

The first step is creating a migration. Migration is a file that will be used to push the model schema changes to the database. The next step is running a command called **migrate,** which will push the model changes to the database using the migrations file and keep both of them in sync. We've discussed this already. So let's do this now for our model – Blog.

This two-step of saving the schema to the database might seem confusing, but it is helpful. Our database might change over time, i.e., adding a new model, creating some new field, or altering an existing field. The migrations help keep track of these changes, so our database and models are always in sync. Let's create the migration for the model we just created by running the following command.

Terminal

```
(MyProject) E:\MyProject\financeblog>>python manage.py makemigrations
```

```
Migrations for 'blog':
  blog\migrations\0001_initial.py
    - Create model Blog
```

You should see a file "**0001_initial.py**" inside the "**migrations**" folder of the blog application. This file will be used to create the schema in our database when we run the following command. Let's push these changes to the database schema by running the "**migrate**" command.

Terminal

```
(MyProject) E:\MyProject\financeblog>>python manage.py migrate
```

```
Operations to perform:
  Apply all migrations: admin, auth, blog, contenttypes, sessions
Running migrations:
  Applying blog.0001_initial... OK
```

Now that we ran the "**migrate**" command, our database schema and our models are in sync. Just note that every time you change your Model attributes or create a new model, you must first run the "**makemigrations**" command, which will allow Django to keep track of the changes. Afterward, you run the "**migrate**" command to make sure your models and database are in sync

ADMIN UI SITE FOR THE PROJECT MANAGEMENT

Django gives us an admin site out of the box that allows us to manage content very quickly. We can create, update and delete model instances in the admin site. The admin site is dynamically generated for a model by reading the model data. We have to use it to register the model we want to be available on our admin site. This is also an application, and Django automatically added it to the "**INSTALLED_APPS**" setting in the "**settings.py**" file.

Let's register our "**Blog**" model with the admin site. Open the "**admin.py**" file inside the "**blog**" application and add the following code:

```python
from django.contrib import admin
from .models import Blog

admin.site.register(Blog)
```

Code 6 financeblog\blog\admin.py

We have registered our "**Blog**" model with the admin site, and it should now be available on the admin site – more on that in the next sections. When your application grows in size, meaning you create many models, it makes sense to pass the model in a list to *admin.site.register()*. You can go a step further and create a method that will extract all models from models.py inside the application and pass them to *...register()*.

CREATING A SUPERUSER

To access the admin site, we need a superuser with admin privileges. Create a superuser by running the "**createsuperuser**" command like so:

Terminal

```
(MyProject) E:\MyProject\financeblog>python manage.py createsuperuser
Username (leave blank to use 'Andrey'): root
Email address: root@gmail.com
Password:
Password (again):
Superuser created successfully.
```

Enter your username, email, and password to create the superuser. Now let's access the admin site.

DJANGO ADMIN SITE

Run the development server and go to http://localhost:8000/admin:

Figure 12 - Blank Django Admin Login Interface

Use the username and password of the user you created earlier to login. You should now see the home page of the Admin site.

Figure 13 - Home Page of a logged in Admin in the Admin UI

You can see models called "**Groups**'' and "**Users**". They are shipped with Django and part of the Django authentication application (**django.contrib.auth**).Django registers these two automatically with the admin site. You can view existing users by clicking on "**Users**", add new users or delete existing users, though currently, only one user exists. We will not be concerned with the "**Groups**" model in this book. Groups are generally used to assign permissions or labels to individual users.

Below these two models, we can see our **Blog** model. It shows up here because we registered it earlier with the admin site. Let's create a new blog entry. Click the "**Add**" button next to *Blogs*. You will see that the Django admin has automatically generated a form for this model:

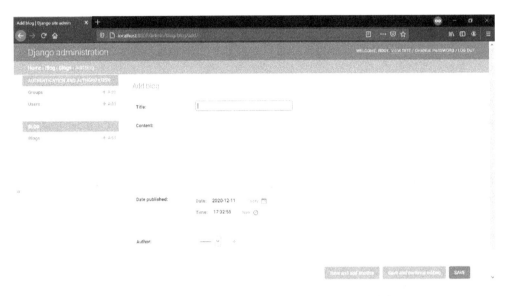

Figure 14 - An input Form for every added and migrated Model

This is great as it gives us a quick and user-friendly way to create, update or delete model instances. If you have ever tried to create an Admin UI (and forms) for your projects, you know how much work and frustration Django liberates you from. Fill the form and save the blog. You should be redirected to a listing page with a success message.

Django 3 for Beginners

Figure 15 - Overview of Model Entries (table rows) in Admin UI

Now experiment with the admin site by adding a few more blogs or users, updating some blogs, or deleting a few of them.

DJANGOS ORM - DJANGO SHELL

THEORY

Django gives us a database-abstraction API that lets us create, update, delete and retrieve objects – the so-called CRUD Operations. This API will take care of writing SQL Queries under the hood. At the same time, we can easily use function calls to perform actions on the database.

This allows every python developer to perform complex CRUD Tasks on a SQL Database without having any experience with SQL.

PRACTICE

Let's take a quick look at the Django Shell. You can think of this shell as a stripped-down version of your Django website. It boots into your Django Project, loads your settings and apps. From there on, you can manage your Project, load models, manipulate the Database, and so on. We'll focus on CRUD Operations for models. Close the server and write the command "**manage.py shell**" to enter the python shell in the context of our project:

Terminal

```
(MyProject) E:\MyProject\financeblog>python manage.py shell
```

CREATING OBJECTS

Now enter the following code:

```
from blog.models import Blog
from django.contrib.auth.models import User
user = User.objects.get(username="root")
blog = Blog(title="Test Blog", content="A test blog...", author=user)
blog.save()
```

Let's take a look at the code in detail. At the top, we are importing our Blog model and Django's default User model.

```
user = User.objects.get(username="root")
```

In this line, we are using the "**get**" method, which returns a single object from the database. If no objects are found matching the query, then it will raise a *DoesNotExist Exception*. Also, note that the get method expects a single object from the database. If your query returns more than one object, it will raise a *MultipleObjectsReturned Exception*.

```
blog = Blog(title="Test Blog", content="A test blog...", author=user)
```

In this line, we are creating a new Blog instance by passing named values in the model. We are not passing in the *"date_published"* value as it gets added automatically upon the creation of the object – re-read the **auto_add_now=True** part. Note that this blog instance has only been created in memory – if you check the Database at this stage, you won't see the new entry.

```
blog.save()
```

This is the line that will actually save the blog instance to our database. It used the INSERT SQL statement to save a new record. To directly save to the database, we can use the create method:

```
Blog.objects.create(title="Hello world", content="Some blog content...", author=user)
```

UPDATING OBJECTS

Let's change the Blog object we created that is stored in our blog variable:

```
blog.title = "Updated blog title"
blog.save()
```

We changed the title of the blog and called the save method. This time it checks whether that record already exists and changes only a part of it. It will perform UPDATE.

Django returns objects from a database in the form of *QuerySet Object*. A *QuerySet* is a collection of objects returned from a database. It offers many filters to limit the results further.

> *A QuerySet Object is the equivalent of the "**SELECT**" SQL statement.*
>
> *Whereas the filters-methods are the limiting clauses such as **WHERE, ORDER BY**, etc..*

We can get a QuerySet by calling a filter method on our model's Manager, "**objects**". To retrieve all objects, we can use the "**all**" method.

```
Blog.objects.all()
    ➤    <QuerySet [<Blog: First Blog>, <Blog: Test Blog>, <Blog: Hello world>]>
```

We can retrieve objects based on a filter. Let's retrieve blogs that start with "Test".

```
Blog.objects.filter(title__startswith="Test")
    ⟍    <QuerySet [<Blog: Test Blog>]>
```

Let's take a look at the commonly used QuerySet filters before moving to the next section. Be aware that the following table is just a subset of all filters. A more complex filter should be researched in the official documentation based on your current Django Installation. The following can be read and executing with the following simple syntax:

```
from .models import model_name
obj_or_queryset = model_name.obejcts.<method_name_from_the_table>()
```

Table 2: QuerySet Methods and Filters

Method name	Description	Returns
filter()	Returns matching Objects based on Field Lookups.	QuerySet
order_by()	Returns matching Objects ordered based on Models Meta-Class or provided field name as parameter.	QuerySet
all()	Basically, it returns a copy of the QuerySet you invocating the method on.	QuerySet
get()	Returns a single Object based on given Field Lookups and parameters.	Model Instance
create()	Creates and returns the newly created Object.	Model Instance
get_or_create()	Tries to fetch a single object based on given Field Lookups and Parameters. If None were found, the Object would be created filled with data that you passed as search criteria.	Model Instance
count()	Counts all the objects based on the searching criteria and returns an integer. Similar to "COUNT()" SQL Statement.	Model Instance
latest()	Returns the latest Object from a QuerySet, based on fields provided as parameters.	Model Instance
first()	Returns the first Object from a QuerySet. The equivalent of fetching the 0th index from a list.	Model Instance
last()	Returns the last Object from a QuerySet. The equivalent of fetching the n-1th index from a list.	Model Instance
delete()	Deletes one Object or all Objects from a QuerySet.	# deleted Obj.

We have learned how to interact with the database and manage our data, and now it is time to move on to creating views for our Blog application.

CREATING VIEWS

THEORY

Django View is a class or a method that receives a web request as an argument and returns a web response. We can return HTML documents, JSON Payloads (think REST API), Images, XML etc. The Business Logic of Django App will reside in the view layer.

You can find many discussions online about where business logic code goes in Django. There many valid suggestions – like outsourcing them in so-called Services – but we will stick with the simplest solution.

Generally, you are free to name your views as you wish and assign them tasks that you deem necessary. But in Django, as is the case in many other web frameworks, you have a handful of Views considered "Standard," which will cover most of your use cases.

Table 3: Django (Generic) View Types

View Name (=Django Class)	Description
DetailView	Used to display detailed data of a model e.g., - a User Profile - single Transaction - single Post
CreateView	Displays a Form with necessary input fields to create a new model e.g., - User Registration - sending Money - publishing a Post
UpdateView	Displays a pre-filled Form with necessary input fields to update an existing model e.g., - Update User Profile - Update or Cancel a Transaction - edit a Post
DeleteView	Used to handle model entry deletions.
ListView	Used to display all or a subset of Entries of (a) model(s). e.g., - List a Users' friends - List of transaction in past 7 days - List of Posts this month

PRACTICE

We will now create a list view and a detailed view. One view will display a list of all the blogs in our database, and the other will display a detailed page of one specific blog.

Django 3 for Beginners

We will first write the logic of these two views, and then we will route them to URL patterns, so Django knows what URL is bound to what view. Lastly, we will create an HTML template that will be returned by our view (function) along with an HTTP response to show the data. Open the "**views.py**" file inside your blog application and write the following code.

```
from django.shortcuts import render, get_object_or_404
from .models import Blog

def list_blogs(request):
    blogs = Blog.objects.all()
    return render(request, "blog/list.html", {"blogs": blogs})
```

Code 7 - financeblog/blog/views.py

We've just created our first view. Our **list_blogs** view takes the **request** as a parameter. Note that **all views require a request**. Afterwards, we are fetching all the blogs and storing them in a variable called **blogs**. Lastly, we are returning the **render** function. The render function takes three parameters: request, a path to our HTML template, and the content dictionary.

CONTENT DICTIONARY

The third parameter to the render function is a dictionary of variables we want to use in our template. In this case, we are passing our **blogs** under the essential *blogs,* and looking back at our Table with *QuerySet* filters, we see that *blogs* should now return a *QuerySet* (=think python list).

The render method is a shortcut function to return an *HttpResponse,* and some data and a template – the type of the returned document is HTML in this case.

A request is an object that Django builds for you – it's an HttpRequest Class instance. Your job is to extract the data from the object needed for your business logic – your view method. Below you'll find a couple of essential and often used attributes and methods of the *HttpRequest* object.

Table 4: Important *HttpRequest* Attributes and Methods

Attributes or Method	Description
HttpRequest.scheme	Returns a string with either 'http' or 'https'
HttpReuqest.body	Returns the raw HTTP Body.
HttpRequest.method	Returns Request Method like 'GET' or 'POST'
HttpRequest.POST	Returns HTTP POST parameters
HttpRequest.GET	Returns HTTP GET parameters

CREATING BLOG DETAIL VIEW

Let's add a detail view down below the **list_blogs** view:

```
def detail_blog(request, pk):
    blog = get_object_or_404(Blog, pk=pk)
    return render(request, "blog/detail.html", {"blog": blog})
```

Code 8 - financeblog/blog/views.py

- This view takes **pk** along with the required **request** parameter. The pk here means *primary key*, and it will be used to retrieve a single Blog record from the database.
- The function called **get_object_or_404**, here we pass a model and a querying parameter to fetch a single record. If the function finds the record, it will return a *QuerySet*. Otherwise, it will display a 404-error page.
- Next, we are returning the render method with a path to our **detail** template and passing the **blog** instance to the template. Let's hook our views with the URL patterns.

URL PATTERNS

THEORY

When a user requests a page on our Django website through a URL, Django will go through a list of URL patterns in the project and stop at the one that matches the user's requested URL.

The URL patterns are concatenated from all applications inside a project, with one *urls.py* file being the central one – **project_name/project_name/urls.py** . In our case, this central urls.py file is located in *financeblog/financeblog/urls.py*. As we will see shortly, in this main file, we'll point to different locations – views and urls.py files of other applications - in our Web App.

The URL pattern will have a View associated with it. Django will run that View and if any parameters are sent with the request, pass them to the View. The response returned by the View will be sent back to the User.

PRACTICE

Create a "**urls.py**" file inside the **blog** application and the following code to create URL patterns for our two views.

```
from django.urls import path
from . import views

urlpatterns = [
    path("", views.list_blogs, name="blog_list"),
    path("blog/<int:pk>", views.detail_blog, name="blogs_detail"),
]
```

Code 9 - financeblog/blog/urls.py

We use the "**path**" function to create a URL pattern. The first argument is the *URL path*, and the second is the view we want to associate with this *URL path pattern and* a named argument called name.

Our first URL pattern is empty and takes no parameters, and is linked to our **list_blogs** view – the one method we defined in the last section. We call it "**blog_list**" and we can use this name inside our project to refer to this URL pattern.

Our second URL path takes an argument – only now our URL path truly becomes a *pattern*. After the keyword "blog/", we pass it a value of type *int*, meaning that it must be a number, and we have given it the name of **pk**. The variable *pk* will be available to us inside the *View* under the name of **pk**. That's why we passed a parameter of "**pk**" to our **blog_detail** view method.

We have to include the URL patterns of our blog application inside our project's main "**urls.py**" file. Open the "**urls.py**" inside the "**financeblog**" directory and put the following:

```
from django.contrib import admin
from django.urls import path, include

urlpatterns = [
    path('admin/', admin.site.urls),
    path('', include('blog.urls'))
]
```

Code 10 - financeblog/financeblog/urls.py

We tell Django to include the URL patterns defined inside the blog application under the "/" path. Since we want to display blogs on our home page where the URL will be localhost:8000/, we don't want to put our blog's URL patterns under the "blog/" path as the "admin/" has done. That is why we are leaving it empty here.

TEMPLATE VIEWS

THEORY

A Template in Django is a file with an ending of ***.html**. This Document is a merger of static HTML Content and dynamic Content supplied by **views.py**. In *views.py,* we pass dynamic data to the template (e.g., User data, Pictures, Menu items, etc.). The passed dynamic data will be a Python dictionary.

Django will look for templates inside the **templates/** directory of each of our applications. Note that Django doesn't differentiate between template directories of different applications. It treats them as if they were all in a single directory.

That is why, for isolation, we create another directory by the name of the application inside the **application_name/templates/** directory and store our template files inside that directory. So, we'll be placing our templates into **blog/templates/blog/**. It's slightly confusing, but we will get there!

Using Django templates, we can do a lot more than just display static HTML files. We can perform

- loops inside our templates,
- conditionals (if, else-if, else),
- inherit from other templates
- and much more.

Django provides a straightforward syntax for the templating engine. We can create and use

- template tags ≈≈ **{% tag_name %}**
- template variables that look like ≈≈ **{{ variable }}**
- template filters that we can call on our variables ≈≈ **{{ variable|filter }}**

Create a **templates** directory inside your blog application. Now create a folder called **blog** inside the templates directory – as explained previously. Lastly, create three HTML files called **base.html** (note that .html is an extension, not part of the name), **list.html**, and **detail.html**. You should have a directory structure inside the blog application like the following figure.

Figure 16 - Templates folder structure for the App 'Blog'

PRACTICE

MAIN PARENT TEMPLATE

The **base.html** will hold content that all of our pages/templates will share

- HTML <head> tag,
- CSS,
- JavaScript CDNs
- Other files
- navigation bar
- etc.

This is the foundation template from which all of our other models will be extracted. Add the following to the **base.html.** Anything that your Web App needs on a global level (say font or icon files) is the place for it.

```
{% load static %}
<!doctype html>
<html lang="en">
  <head>
    <meta charset="utf-8">
    <meta name="viewport" content="width=device-width, initial-scale=1, shrink-to-fit=no">
    <link rel="stylesheet" href="https://cdn.jsdelivr.net/npm/bootstrap@4.5.3/dist/css/bootstrap.min.css" integrity="sha384-TX8t27EcRE3e/ihU7zmQxVncDAy5uIKz4rEkgIXeMed4M0jlfIDPvg6uqKI2xXr2" crossorigin="anonymous">
    <link rel="preconnect" href="https://fonts.gstatic.com">
    <link href="https://fonts.googleapis.com/css2?family=Poppins:wght@400;600;700&display=swap" rel="stylesheet">
    <link rel="stylesheet" type="text/css" href="{% static 'blog/main.css' %}">
    <title>My Finance Blog</title>
  </head>
  <body class="bg-light">
<header>
    <nav class="navbar navbar-expand-lg navbar-dark bg-dark">
        <div class="container">
            <a class="navbar-brand mb-0 h1" href="{% url 'blog_list' %}">My Financial Blog</a>
        </div>
    </nav>
</header>
{% block content %}
{% endblock content %}
    <script src="https://code.jquery.com/jquery-3.5.1.min.js" integrity="sha256-9/aliU8dGd2tb60SsuzixeV4y/faTqgFtohetphbbj0=" crossorigin="anonymous"></script>
```

```
    <script src="https://cdn.jsdelivr.net/npm/bootstrap@4.5.3/dist/js/bootstrap.bundle.min
.js" integrity="sha384-
ho+j7jyWK8fNQe+A12Hb8AhRq26LrZ/JpcUGGOn+Y7RsweNrtN/tE3MoK7ZeZDyx" crossorigin="anonymous">
</script>
    <script src="https://cdn.jsdelivr.net/npm/js-
cookie@rc/dist/js.cookie.min.js"></script>

  </body>
</html>
```

Code 11 - financeblog/blog/templates/blog/base.html

This is just a simple bootstrap HTML document. We've included the bootstrap CSS, js, jquery, and a js-cookie library via CDN. To load local static files such as CSS and js files, we have to call the "**{% load static %}**" template tag at the top of our document, which is what we have done here. This gives us access to the "**{% static "path_to_file" %}**" template tag. Find the **link** tag in the head tag:

```
<link rel="stylesheet" type="text/css" href="{% static 'blog/main.css' %}">
```

You can see it is using the **static** template tag and looking for a **main.css** file. Let's add the **main.css** file. Create the following directory structure inside the **blog** application.

Figure 17 - Folder Structure for Static Django Assets

As you can see, we apply the same structure to **static/** directories as we did to **templates/** directories. So, what is happening here is following: with the 'static' template tag, we tell Django to replace the

128

```
{% static 'blog/main.css' %}
```

Part with a working path pointing to our Django static folder in the blog application – more specifically, the static asset *main.css*. I assume you hate CSS – I've heard some backend developers do – so we will skip this part. Please copy the *main.css* from the GitHub repo into the previously mentioned location in your App. Otherwise, you may go through the *main.css* yourself or create your styles.

Terminal

```
wget https://raw.githubusercontent.com/AndreyBulezyuk/Django-3-
Book/master/blog/static/blog/main.css
```

The navbar logo links to our **list_blog** view's URL using the **{% url 'blog_list' %}** template tag.

TEMPLATE BLOCKS AND INHERITANCE

After the header tag in the body of the *base.html*, you should've noticed the **{% block %}** tag. We can name our *block template tags,* and we are calling it "content", so it becomes **{% block content %}**.

This template tag will create a block in our document. Templates that inherit from this **base.html** template can fill this block with data, tags, or comments. Note that the block template tag has a closing tag called "**{% endblock %}**". Let's edit the template of our **list_blog** view, which is located at **templates>blog>list.html** inside the blog application.

```
{% extends "blog/base.html" %}

{% block content %}

<div class="landing bg-dark">
    <div class="container">
        <div class="row align-items-center justify-content-center">
            <div class="col-sm-12 col-lg-6 text-center">
                <h1 class="text-white font-weight-bold display-3 mb-
3">Finance blogs to help you succeed.</h1>

            </div>
        </div>
    </div>
</div>

<div class="container p-5 rounded ">
    {% for blog in blogs %}
        <div class="row blog mb-5">
            <div class="col-lg-2 col-sm-12 text-center">
                <a class="mugshot-container mb-1" href="#">
                    <span>{{blog.author.username}}</span>
                </a>
                <small class="text-
muted">{{blog.date_published|date:"d/m/Y h:i a"}}</small>
            </div>
            <div class="col-lg-10 col-sm-12">
                <div class="blog-information">
                    <h1 class="font-weight-bold mb-3">{{blog.title}}</h1>
                    <p>{{blog.content|truncatewords:30}}</p>
                    <a href="{% url 'blogs_detail' blog.pk %}" class="font-weight-bold mb-
3 d-inline-block">
                        Read More
                    </a>
                </div>
            </div>
        </div>
    {% endfor %}
</div>
{% endblock content %}
```

Code 12 financeblog\blog\templates\blog\list.html

At the top, we are using the **extends** template tag to tell Django that this template inherits from the *base.html* template. Next, we are adding content to the **content block** we created in *base.html*.

We are looping over the **blogs** list we passed to this template through the view and display the blog title, author of the blog, published date of the blog, and body of the blog. The following picture visualizes the way list.html and base.html will work together.

130

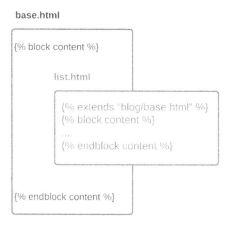

base.html

{% block content %}

list.html

{% extends "blog/base.html" %}
{% block content %}
...
{% endblock content %}

{% endblock content %}

Figure 18 - Template extends tag, similar to Parent-Child Relationship

We are also adding a link to the *detail_blog* view using the **url template tag** i.e. "{% url 'blogs_detail' blog.pk %}". We are passing it the pk (primary key) of the blog object as required in our **blog_detail** view.

By default, Django date fields display time and date, but we wanted to display only the date and in a specific format. For that, we used the date template filter on the **date_published** field.

We have also used a template filter on the content of the body, *"{{blog.content|truncatewords:30}}"*, called **truncatewords**. This template filter limits the word count of our blogs' content and will only display up to 30 words. If the user wants to read more, they can visit the detail page of that specific blog.

So, let's edit the template of our *detail_blog* view which is located at **templates>blog>detail.html** inside the blog application:

```
{% extends "blog/base.html" %}
{% block content %}
<div class="container blog bg-light p-5 mt-5 rounded ">
    <div class="row">
        <div class="col-3 text-center">
            <a class="mugshot-container mb-1" href="#">
                <span>{{blog.author.username}}</span>
            </a>
            <small class="text-muted">{{blog.publish_date|date:"d/m/Y h:i a"}}</small>
        </div>
        <div class="col-9 question-information pb-1">
            <h1 class="blog-card-title mb-3 font-weight-bold">{{blog.title}}</h1>
        </div>
    </div>
    <div class="row">
      <div class="col-12 mt-5">
        <p class="line-height text-justify"> {{blog.content}}</p>
      </div>
    </div>
</div>
{% endblock content %}
```

Code 13 financeblog\blog\templates\blog\detail.html

We are doing the same thing as we have done with the **list.html** template. We are extending from the *base.html* template. We are then opening the content block and filling it with content. Unlike the *list* template, which receives **a list of Blog objects**, the *detail template* receives only **a single Blog object**. That is the reason we are not performing any loops here.

RESULTS

Make sure your development server is running and open http://localhost:8000:

Figure 19 - List Template Top Page

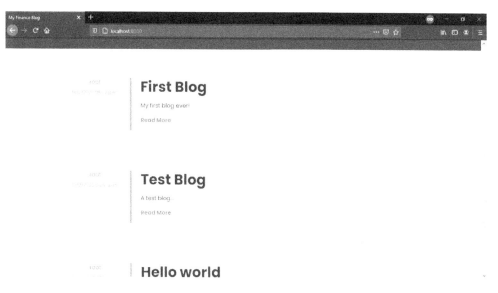

Figure 20 - List Template Blog Display

On the homepage of our website, you can now see a heading and a list of blogs. This is the **list_blog** view. We show the date a blog was created, who created the blog, the blog's title, a short description of the blog, and a "read more" button that will lead you to the **detail_blog** view of a specific blog.

Note the URL of a blog's detail page, and it has a number after the "blog/". This number here is the **pk** of a blog instance and will be passed to our view, and our view will then use it to find a blog object instance – see code on page 123. If found, it will return to this page. Otherwise, we will be shown a 404 error. Click the **"read more"** button of any of the blogs, and it will lead you to that blog's specific detail page.

Figure 21 - Detail Template

Albeit very minimal, we now have a working blogging site where users can read blogs. The homepage lists the available blogs, and each blog has a detail page.

Let's recap what we have just done with the following simplified (and intentionally incomplete) representation. The flow starts with the request being routed via **urls.py** to the right view. In **views.py** the right view is being invoked. The business logic is applied (like CRUD Operations on Models), and the template is rendered.

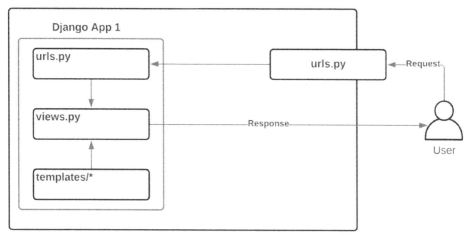

Figure 22 - Simplified Representation of the Request Flow

So, in essence, whenever you need to add a browsable page to your Django Project, this is roughly the process you have to go through. Our website is far from finished. Let's expand our application's functionalities in the next chapter.

APPLICATION

We did pretty well so far. This chapter will create a new application, repeating some steps from the previous Chapter while injecting new ones. For example, we will learn how to use new Field Types in models, create Forms and use a Django feature called "Signals."

Right now, our blog application has a minimal set of functionalities – not useful for anything. Only a superuser can create blogs through the admin site. We want regular users to post blogs, but we don't want regular users to access our admin site.

We have no register, login, or logout functionalities on our site yet. In this chapter, we will create all the components that these functionalities consist of. With that in place, new users can register on our website.

NEW PROFILES APPLICATION

THEORY

We want to give our users the ability to have a profile picture and post a short description about themselves. If you remember, Django gives us a *User* model out of the box, but it doesn't have an image or a description field. We can either extend the existing User model or create another model called *Profile* and give it a One-to-One relationship with the *User* model.

We will go with the latter approach as it is the preferred way. This approach is preferred because we won't have to re-code many built-in functionalities of the built-in *User* model (e.g., login, register, etc.). Also, this will prevent unintended

136

consequences down the road, e.g., when applying a Django update that alters the User model in some way. You'll see a simple Class Diagram displaying the relationship between our two models in the below figure.

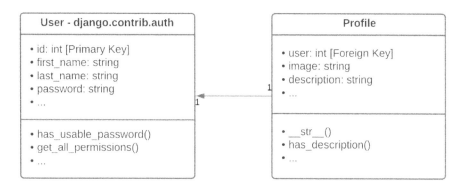

Figure 23 - One-to-One Relationship between Django-supplied User and manually-created Profile model

PRACTICE

CREATING AN APPLICATION

Let's create an application called **profiles**. Close the server, go to the root directory of the project, and type the following command.

Terminal

```
(MyProject) E:\MyProject\financeblog>python manage.py startapp profiles
```

Running this command should create a "profiles" application for us. We will put every User related feature in this application. Let's register this application within our current project. Open the *settings.py* file of the project inside **financeblog/** and add the name of our application to the **INSTALLED_APPS** list.

```
INSTALLED_APPS = [
    'django.contrib.admin',
    'django.contrib.auth',
    'django.contrib.contenttypes',
    'django.contrib.sessions',
    'django.contrib.messages',
    'django.contrib.staticfiles',
    'blog',
    'profiles'
]
```

Code 14 financeblog\financeblog\settings.py

On server restart, Django will be loading the source code profiles application. Then we create a couple of new entries and, before that, a migration.

CREATING MODEL

As stated before, Django's built-in *User* model does not provide an image or a description field. That's why we will create a new model called Profile and give it an image and a description field. We will then give it a one-to-one relationship with the *User* model to only have one Profile and vice versa.

This Profile Model is the place for further fields for your App Users. One could imagine fields like 'LinkedIn Profile', 'Instagram Page', 'Phone Number', 'Years of Experience in Django' to be at the right place in Profile. Your Users Payment Methods, on the other hand, would be best outsourced into another model.

Add the following code to the **models.py** file of the newly created **profiles** application.

```
from django.db import models
from django.contrib.auth.models import User

class Profile(models.Model):
    user = models.OneToOneField(User, on_delete=models.CASCADE)
    image = models.ImageField(default="default.jpg", upload_to="profile_pictures")
    description = models.CharField(max_length=500, blank=True)

    def __str__(self):
        return f'{self.user.username}\'s Profile...'
```

Code 15 financeblog\profiles\models.py

Let's go over the fields:

- **user:** We are defining a One-to-One Relationship with the *User* model, i.e., one user can only have one profile and vice versa.
- **description**: It is a simple *CharField*. We are setting *blank* to True because we don't want to force our users to write a description about themselves if they don't want to. One can think of setting the *default* parameter to something like "This profile has no description yet".
- **image:** We are defining an ImageField type. Django doesn't store images as binary data in the database. It stores them on the file system and saves a path in the database field. We are specifying a default Image; in case the user doesn't upload one. In *upload_to,* we set a path where to store the Images: *profile_pictures/*. By default, Django will store user uploaded files defined by the **MEDIA_URL** and **MEDIA_ROOT** settings (more in the next Section).

You can also do some minor database optimizations by omitting the default parameter for specific fields.

Take description as an example. You could provide a default value that is about 1KB in size. If you have 100.000 Entries with a default value, you are adding 100 MB to your DB. In this scenario, it's advised to create a model method (just like we created *__str__()* to return the necessary default information if the field is empty.

APPLYING MODEL TO DATABASE

Note: Our environment needs the package "Pillow" to work with Images in Django. Otherwise, you might get an Error while creating migrations in the next Paragraph. The Exception will look like this:

Terminal

```
SystemCheckError: System check identified some issues:

ERRORS:

profiles.Profile.image: (fields.E210) Cannot use ImageField because Pillow is not
installed.

    HINT: Get Pillow at https://pypi.org/project/Pillow/ or run command "python -m
pip install Pillow".

(MyProject) E:\MyProject\financeblog>pip install Pillow
```

Remember the steps from page 99 and try to migrate this new app on your own before proceeding with the following code. Let's create the migrations for this model and push these schema changes to our database.

Terminal

```
(MyProject) E:\MyProject\financeblog>python manage.py makemigrations
Migrations for 'profiles':
  profiles\migrations\0001_initial.py
    - Create model Profile

(MyProject) E:\MyProject\financeblog>python manage.py migrate
Operations to perform:
  Apply all migrations: admin, auth, blog, contenttypes, profiles, sessions
Running migrations:
  Applying profiles.0001_initial... OK
```

CONFIGURING MEDIA SERVER PATHS

We need to configure the **MEDIA_URL** and **MEDIA_ROOT** settings to specify where our images are saved and under what path we have them available. Open the **settings.py** and add the following code:

```
import os
MEDIA_ROOT = os.path.join(BASE_DIR, 'media')
MEDIA_URL = '/media/'
```

Code 16 financeblog\financeblog\settings.py

We are importing the os module and using it to set the **MEDIA_ROOT** to a directory called **media** in our project's root directory. Next, we define the **MEDIA_URL**, so any user uploaded files will become available to us under the path "**media/**" after the domain of the site.

To serve user uploaded files during development, we have to add the following change to the **urls.py** file of the project inside the **financeblog** directory:

```
from django.contrib import admin
from django.urls import path, include
from django.conf import settings
from django.conf.urls.static import static
urlpatterns = [
    path('admin/', admin.site.urls),
    path('', include('blog.urls'))
]
urlpatterns += static(settings.MEDIA_URL, document_root=settings.MEDIA_ROOT)
```

Code 17 financeblog\financeblog\urls.py

Here we are building the path for our files, and we are making them available under the path "**/media/**" which we have given to the **MEDIA_URL** setting. Do note that this is not the preferred way of serving files in production.

We have configured our Django project's settings to upload profile pictures, but we haven't created the directories for it. In the root directory of the project, create a directory called **media**. Inside it, put a jpg image by the name "default.jpg" and create a folder called **profile_pictures**.

The **default.jpg** image is for when the user doesn't upload an image themselves. The **profile_pictures** is the directory where the user-uploaded images will actually be saved. You should now have the following directory structure for the **media** directory inside the root directory of the project:

```
∨ media
  > profile_pictures
    default.jpg
```

TESTING THE PROFILE MODEL

REGISTER THE PROFILE MODEL

Open the **admin.py** file inside the **profiles** application and add the following code to register our **Profile** model to the admin site:

```
from django.contrib import admin
from .models import Profile
admin.site.register(Profile)
```

Code 18 financeblog\profiles\admin.py

Make sure the development server is running and head over to http://localhost:8000/admin and log in. Click on the profiles link, and it should lead you to the following page. Why would you not want to include a model/entity into the admin site UI? Because some models are supposed to be background only (e.g. Logging, Backup Tracking, …).

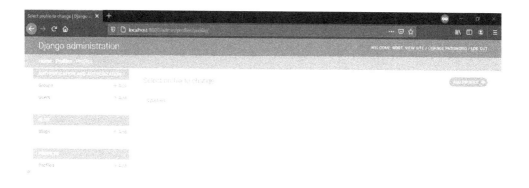

Figure 24 Admin side UI

As you can see, there aren't any **Profile** objects yet. We only have a single user in our database right now, i.e., the superuser root.

CREATING AND ASSOCIATING A NEW PROFILE

Let's create the **root**'s profile. Click the "**Add Profile**':

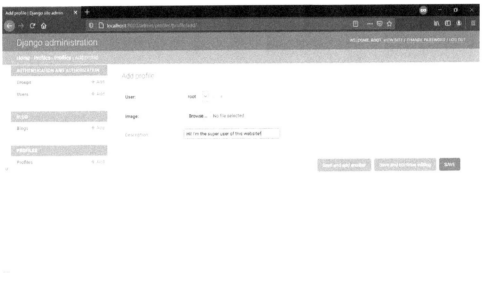

Figure 25 Adding a profile

I've purposefully left the image field blank. Click save, and it should lead you to the following page:

Django 3 for Beginners

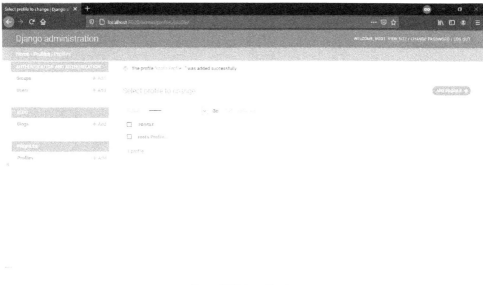

Figure 26 List profile view

Interestingly Django makes an effort to adjust the name of the object so that the one-to-one relationship between user and profile becomes apparent. I'm talking about the "root's Profile". Let's click on the Profile we just created, and it should show you the following.

Figure 27 root profile view

As you can see, since we didn't explicitly set an image for the profile, it chose a default image as we specified in our **models.py** file. Clicking on the image will show you the image.

Figure 28 Uploaded Image view in web

Note the URL of the image is pointing to the "media/" path. Everything works perfectly. We can now create a view, templates and display this stuff on the main website, but we have to take care of a minor problem first.

PROBLEM WITH THE PROFILE MODEL

DISCOVERING THE (FORESEEABLE) ISSUE

Let's add a new user through the admin site. Open the admin site and click the **add** link next to **User:**

Django 3 for Beginners

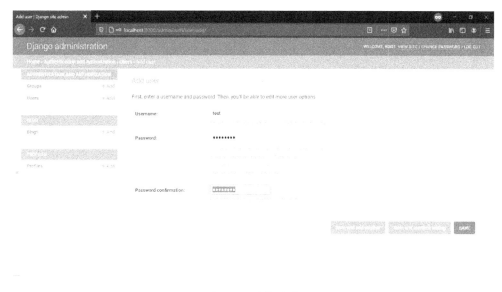

Figure 29 Adding link

After you have added the user successfully, go to the Profiles section in the admin site:

Figure 30 Profile Section in Admin Site

The profile for our newly created user was not created automatically. Remember, the **Profile** is a separate model and only shares a one-to-one relationship with the **User** model. This one-to-one relationship is set to one column/attribute only. This does not force a new profile entry to be created in a database when a new User is being created.

SOLUTION

We want a new profile to be created automatically when a user is created and associate it with the new user. Luckily, there's something called Django Signals which can help us in this situation.

DJANGO SIGNALS

EMIT AND LISTEN - SEND AND RECEIVE

Using Django signals, we can allow applications to be notified when an action occurs. In simple terms, we will create a receiver in our application whose job is to listen for signals. Django will emit signals whenever something is done in our application. We can tell our receiver function **what signal it should listen to**.

For example, using the **post_save** signal and a **receiver**, we can be notified whenever the **User** model is created. We can automate the process of creating a **Profile** for that newly created User.

AUTOMATING THE CREATION OF PROFILE

Open the **models.py** file of your **profiles** application and make the following changes, so your **models.py** file looks like this:

```
from django.db import models
from django.contrib.auth.models import User
#NEW CODE BELOW
from django.db.models.signals import post_save
from django.dispatch import receiver
#NEW CODE ABOVE

class Profile(models.Model):
    user = models.OneToOneField(User, on_delete=models.CASCADE)
    image = models.ImageField(default="default.jpg", upload_to="profile_pictures")
    description = models.CharField(max_length=500, blank=True)

    def __str__(self):
        return f'{self.user.username}\'s Profile...'

#NEW CODE BELOW
@receiver(post_save, sender=User)
def create_profile(sender, instance, created, **kwargs):
    if created:
        Profile.objects.create(user=instance)
#NEW CODE ABOVE
```

Code 19 financeblog\profiles\models.py

We are importing a signal called **post_save**. Next, we are importing a function called the **receiver**.

Below our **Profile** model, we have created a function called **create_profile** that is decorated by the **receiver** function. The **receiver** function takes two parameters. The first one specifies a signal, and the second one takes the **User** model. It means that whenever a User model has been saved, Django will emit a Signal which we want to receive. After receiving the Django Signal, we are calling the **create_profile** function and executing our business logic.

Our **receiver** function passes several arguments to the **create_profile** function. The **created** parameter is a boolean value that tells us whether the sender object was created or updated. Inside the **create_profile** function body, we create a Profile object and set its user field to the **User** that was just created. We put our signals and receivers inside the **models.py** file of the application Profile.

VERIFYING THE RESULTS

Now open the admin site and delete the test user we previously created:

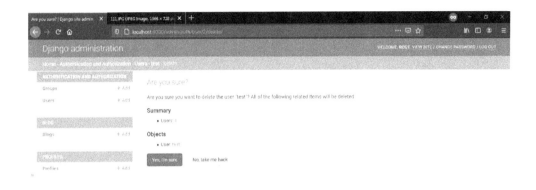

Figure 31 Deleting User

Now add a new user as described on previous pages and call it - again - test. After creating the user successfully, go to the Profiles page in the admin site to verify that the signal received successfully and the profile was created.

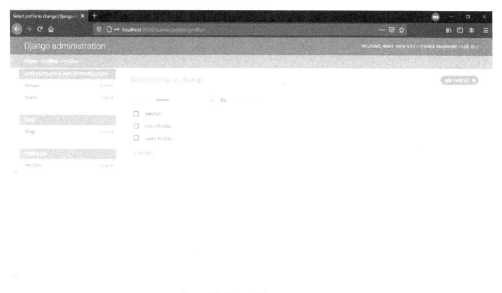

Figure 32 After adding a new user

You can see that Django automatically created the **Profile** of the **User** test we just created. We don't have to worry about creating profiles manually, as those will get created automatically whenever a user is created.

DELETE PROFILE AUTOMATICALLY

Just as we want the Profile of each user to be created automatically, we want each Profile to be deleted when a user is deleted. Let's check if that behavior is already implemented by deleting a random (non-superuser) user. I created manually a User Account for myself. Now let's delete it inside Django shell:

```
>>> python manage.py shell

>>> from django.contrib.auth.models import User

>>> andrey = User.objects.get(pk=2)

>>> andrey

<User: Andrey_Bulezyuk>

>>> andrey.delete()

(2, {'profiles.Profile': 1, 'auth.User': 1})

>>> exit()
```

As the output of "andrey.delete()" already indicates, two objects were deleted: profile. Profile and auth.User. This means that Profile is being deleted automatically when a User Account is deleted. As a refresher: this logic is not covered with a Signal but with the one-to-one relationship in the **Profile** model. To be more precise, it's the **on_delete** parameter.

```
user = models.OneToOneField(User, on_delete=models.CASCADE)
```

ACCOUNT CREATION

Now that our **Profile** model is working correctly, we create a register page so that users can create a new account on our website. Let's see how we can accept user data in Django.

ACCEPTING USER INPUT USING FORMS

We use Django's Form system to accept user input. Using Django forms, we can easily define our form fields and conveniently display them on the template very quickly. We can collect data from users and validate it in our view with the **is_valid** method. If errors are found, then the user is sent back to the form with error messages.

When the validation is done, we have access to all the data submitted by the user in a **cleaned_data** dictionary on the form instance. We can then perform further actions on the validated data - e.g.: apply further business logic.

By default, Django provides two base form classes, i.e., **forms.Form** and **forms.ModelForm**. We create our forms by inheriting from either of the two. Kind of like models, the attributes of our form class will represent a field in the HTML form.

DJANGO FORMS.FORM

If we extend from **forms.Form**, we get an empty skeleton form where we have to configure everything ourselves, from creating fields and field types to handling data after it's validated inside the view. This is suitable when we are not doing anything that directly affects a model, for example, creating a newsletter or a contact us form.

DJANGO FORMS.MODELFORM

On the other hand, if we extend from **forms.ModelForm**, we will have a form tied to a specific model. The form fields are automatically generated for us based on the model we provide our form. But we can configure the premade fields as we need. This form also gives us a **save** method, which will automatically save or update an instance of the model to the database if form fields were validated. A form created using **ModelForm** will validate its field based on the fields that are defined in the model itself. We can, however, if, for some reason, we want our form fields of a model, validate the fields differently from the definitions defined in the model itself.

REGISTER FORM

Create a file called **forms.py** inside the **profiles** application and add the following code:

```
from django import forms
from django.contrib.auth.forms import UserCreationForm
from django.contrib.auth.models import User

class RegisterForm(UserCreationForm):
    first_name = forms.CharField(max_length=50, required=True)
    last_name = forms.CharField(max_length=50, required=True)
    email = forms.EmailField(required=True)

    class Meta:
        model = User
        fields = ['email', 'username', 'first_name', 'last_name', 'password1', 'password2'
]
```

Code 20 financeblog\profiles\forms.py

This is our registration form. Note that our **RegisterForm** class is not inheriting from either **Form** or **ModelForm**. Instead, it is inheriting from a class called **UserCreationForm**. As stated earlier, Django provides an authentication system out of the box which has a User model. Django also provides a form for creating the mentioned User that takes care of various validations such as checking the passwords etc. Under the hood, this **UserCreationForm** class inherits from **ModelForm**.

We could have used this **UserCreationForm** as is in our view. The form would still work just fine. But the form would only show **username, password,** and **password confirmation** fields on our registration page. These are the required fields of Django's User model as defined in its model definitions.

However, we also want to show the other optional fields of the User model, which are **first_name, last_name,** and **email**. We also want to make them **required**. That is why we are further configuring the **UserCreationForm**.

We define the fields first_name and last_name and set their type to **CharField** and their **required** attribute to **True**. We are also defining **email** (type: **EmailField**) and also setting its **required** attribute to **True**. As stated earlier, these fields are not required in Django's **User** model, and the user can leave them blank. However, we want to require these fields so a user can't leave them empty. That is the only reason we are redefining them.

MODELFORM META CLASS

Informs inheriting from **ModelForm,** we have to define a **Meta** class inside the form class. The Meta class must define the attribute called **model** to pass the model we want our form to be built for.

Optionally, we can define the attribute **fields**, which must be a list of fields from the model. If we don't provide this field, ModelForm will build a form with every field from the model.

Django's User model also has other fields like **is_active, is_staff, is_superuser,** etc. We don't want to display them in the form. That is why we are only including the six fields in the **fields** attribute. Those are the fields that we want to be displayed on the registration page. Now that we have created a form. Let us build a view for our **register** page.

CREATING USER REGISTER VIEW

Open **views.py** inside the **profiles** application and add the following code:

```
from django.shortcuts import render, redirect
from .forms import RegisterForm

def register(request):
    if request.method == "POST":
        form = RegisterForm(request.POST)
        if form.is_valid():
            form.save()
            return redirect('blog_list')
    else:
        form = RegisterForm()
    return render(request, "profiles/register.html", {"form": form})
```

Code 21 financeblog\profiles\views.py

We are creating a view called **register**. We are checking whether the request performed by the client is a POST request or not. Whenever we open a link or visit a page, we perform a GET request, but when we submit a form to a webpage, we are performing a POST request. That is what we are checking here through the **request.method** value.

If the request method is POST, we are instantiating an instance of the **RegisterForm**, and passing it the data the user sent through the form on the website, which is available to us under **request.POST**.

Afterward, we are calling the is_valid method of our RegisterForm. It will perform default validation of the fields defined in our form or any custom validation we might have added. If the data submitted by the user is valid and doesn't cause any errors, we are executing the save method. This method will create a new User in the database.

Note that this save method only comes with forms that inherit from ModelForm. The reason we used UserCreationForm is that it also adds other validation for us such as checking the password length and matching if the two passwords match or not.

Once the form is saved and a new user is created, we are using the function redirect, which will redirect us to another page. We pass it the URL name of our blog list view that we defined in its URL pattern (finanaceblog/blog/urls.py).

```
path("", views.list_blogs, name="blog_list"),
```

If the request performed by the user/client is not POST, meaning they opened the register page on their browser (remember this is a GET request as they haven't sent any data), we are instantiating an empty instance of the RegisterForm.

Lastly, we are returning the render method with the template we want our view to link with and pass our **form** to the template.

URL PATTERN FOR REGISTER VIEW

Now that the register view has been created, we have to define its URL pattern. Unlike we did with the **blog** application where we created a separate URLs file inside the application, we will include the URL patterns of our **profiles** application directly in the **urls.py** file of the project. That is because we want to show these URL patterns right after the domain name and not under some path like "/accounts" or "/profiles".

Open the **urls.py** of the project inside the **financeblog** directory and add the following import.

```
from profiles import views as profiles_views
```

Here we are importing the views of our **profiles** application as **profile_views**. Next, add the following URL pattern to the **urlpatterns** list:

```
path('register/', profiles_views.register, name="register")
```

Here we are defining a URL pattern to our register view under the path "register/".
We have given it the name **register**. Just to make things clear, this is how the **urls.py**
file of your **financeblog** directory should look like after making the changes above:

```
from django.contrib import admin
from django.urls import path, include
from django.conf import settings
from django.conf.urls.static import static
#NEW CODE BELOW
from profiles import views as profiles_views
#NEW CODE ABOVE
urlpatterns = [
    path('admin/', admin.site.urls),
    path('', include('blog.urls')),
    # user related paths below
    path('register/', profiles_views.register, name="register")
    # user related paths above
]
urlpatterns += static(settings.MEDIA_URL, document_root=settings.MEDIA_ROOT)
```

Code 22 financeblog\financeblog\urls.py

CREATING TEMPLATE FOR THE REGISTER VIEW

Inside the **profiles** application, create the following directory structure:

This **register.html** file is what our register view will look for based on its render
function's path. Add the following markup to the **register.html** we just created:

158

```
{% extends "blog/base.html" %}
{% block content %}
<div class="landing bg-dark">
    <div class="container">
        <div class="row align-items-center justify-content-center">
            <div class="col-sm-12 col-lg-6 text-center">
                <h1 class="text-white font-weight-bold display-3 mb-3">Register</h1>

            </div>

        </div>

    </div>
</div>
<div class="container bg-light mt-n5 p-5 rounded ">
    <div class="row">
        <div class="col-12">
            <form method="POST">
                {% csrf_token %}
                {{form.as_p}}
                <div class="form-group">
                    <button class="btn btn-outline-dark">Submit</button>
                </div>
                <a href="#">Login?</a>
            </form>
        </div>
    </div>
</div>
{% endblock content %}
```

Code 23 financeblog\profiles\templates\profiles\register.html

Just as we did with the blog detail and blog list view, we are inheriting from the
base.html template. Next, we are opening the **content blocks** and adding our
content between the tags. We are creating a heading that says "Register". Lastly, we
are creating the form with the method set to "POST" because by default, the default
method of HTML forms is GET.

Inside the form, we are calling the **csrf_token** template tag. This token is used to
ensure that the form was sent and created by one of the trusted hosts defined under
the ALLOWED_HOSTS setting. Whenever dealing with forms, you have to use this
template tag. Otherwise, you will get a 403 forbidden error.

Next, we put our form variable inside the HTML form by simply calling the **as_p** method on it. This will automatically output the form fields inside our html form. The **as_p** method will wrap our fields inside a paragraph tag before outputting them to the markup.

Note that the form variable will only create the input fields, we have to create the submit button and the html form wrapper additionally. We have also created a **Login** link at the bottom that currently doesn't lead you anywhere as we have yet to create a login page.

VERIFYING THE REGISTER VIEW RESULTS

Open http://localhost:8000/register and you should see the following:

Figure 33 Register View

You can see that just outputting the **form** variable created all of these fields for us. It also added some helper text that comes with the User model by default. Now try adding some information to the form and submit it. I will intentionally submit the incorrect data to show you that the validation works.

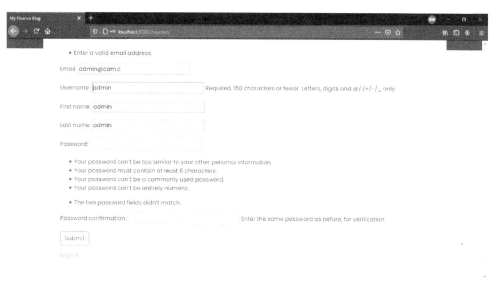

Figure 34 Intentionally wrong data fillup

I supplied an invalid email address and wrote different passwords in the password and password confirmation fields. You can see that it is printing the errors "Enter a valid email address" and "The two passwords don't match". Perfect, the validation works. We can be sure that all User Accounts will have a certain degree of data quality.

Now let's input correct data and try creating a user. If we are successful, we should get redirected to the homepage where all of our blogs are listed. I will create a user, **john.**

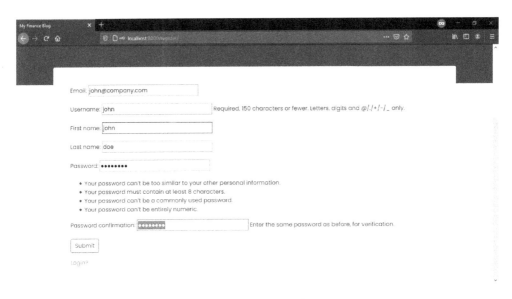

Figure 35 Filling correct data

I was successfully redirected to the homepage. It means our User was created. Open the admin site and make sure that john's **User** Object and john's **Profile** Object do exist.

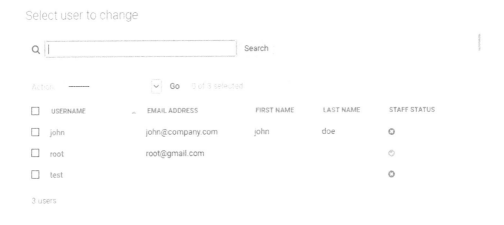

Figure 36 User list

ADDING DJANGO PLUGIN "CRISPY FORMS"

Our register page works fine, but the form doesn't look good at all. We are not controlling the markup of the fields, errors, and helper text ourselves. Instead, we are leaving it up to Django ModelForm.

We can gain more control by looping over the form variable and handling how to display each field and related data such as errors. But that would be too time-consuming if our goal is simply to have fields that look more organized. Luckily we have a package called **django-crispy forms** that will automatically convert our forms to bootstrap forms. Close the development server and install the package through the following command.

Terminal

```
(MyProject) E:\MyProject\financeblog>pip install django-crispy-forms
```

Open the **settings.py** file of the project and add the crispy form App to INSTALLED_APPS. Your list of installed apps should look like this:

```
INSTALLED_APPS = [
    'django.contrib.admin',
    'django.contrib.auth',
    'django.contrib.contenttypes',
    'django.contrib.sessions',
    'django.contrib.messages',
    'django.contrib.staticfiles',
    'blog',
    'profiles',
    'crispy_forms',
]
```

Figure 37 financeblog\financeblog\settings.py

Also, add the following setting in the **settings.py** file:

```
CRISPY_TEMPLATE_PACK = 'bootstrap4'
```

django-crispy-form will use this setting to convert our Django forms to bootstrap 4 templates which is what we are using. Now open the **register.html** inside the **profiles** application under the path **templates > profiles > register.html** and add the following template tag at the top after the **extends** template tag:

```
{% load crispy_forms_tags %}
```

We are loading the template tags of the package we just installed through this template tag. Now in the same file, scroll down to where we are outputting our form as **{{form.as_p}}** and change it to:

```
{{form|crispy}}
```

We have removed the **as_p** method and are now calling the **crispy** filter on our **form** variable. Now your **register.html** file should look like this:

```
{% extends "blog/base.html" %}
{% load crispy_forms_tags %}
{% block content %}
<div class="landing bg-dark">
    <div class="container">
        <div class="row align-items-center justify-content-center">
            <div class="col-sm-12 col-lg-6 text-center">
                <h1 class="text-white font-weight-bold display-3 mb-3">Register</h1>

            </div>
        </div>
    </div>
</div>
<div class="container bg-light mt-n5 p-5 rounded ">
    <div class="row">
        <div class="col-12">
            <form method="POST">
                {% csrf_token %}
                {{form|crispy}}
                <div class="form-group">
                    <button class="btn btn-outline-dark">Submit</button>
                </div>
                <a href="#">Login?</a>
            </form>
        </div>
    </div>
</div>
{% endblock content %}
```

Code 24 financeblog\profiles\templates\profiles\register.html

Run the development server and validate that the register page works as intended. Create a couple of new accounts and test the limits, required fields, lengths, etc.

Figure 38 Updated register page

You can see that our form now looks completely different - definitely better. The **crispy** template filter that we applied to our form will render our form according to bootstrap 4 classes now defined in the **settings.py** file in the setting CRISPY_TEMPLATE_PACK.

Figure 39 Crispy Template filter effect

Another obvious point is that the error messages are highlighted and attract attention to correct the inputs.

DJANGO MESSAGES FRAMEWORK

Our register view works. The forms look great. There is just one thing left to complete it, and these are flash messages. In web applications, a flash message is a one-time message shown to the user once they perform some action, e.g. user either created something or deleted something. We will show them a message whether it was successful or not.

In our case, we want to display a one-time message after the user has successfully registered. Django has a **message** system that allows us to do this very quickly. Open the **views.py** file of the **profiles** application and add the following import to import django's message framework:

```
from django.contrib import messages
```

Next, in the **register** view, add the following line of code right before the **redirect** function call after we are calling the **save** method on the form:

```
messages.success(request, "User created successfully!")
```

We are creating a flash message, and it is of type **success**. We have different types of messages, e.g., info, warning, etc. You can use it to determine what sort of styles you want to apply for different kinds of messages on the template. The first parameter is always the request object, and the second parameter is our message we want to show. After making the changes, this is how your register view should look like:

```
def register(request):
    if request.method == "POST":
        form = RegisterForm(request.POST)
        if form.is_valid():
            form.save()
            messages.success(request, "User created successfully!")
            return redirect('blog_list')
    else:
        form = RegisterForm()
    return render(request, "profiles/register.html", {"form": form})
```

Code 25 financeblog/profiles/views.py

Open the **base.html** file inside **templates>blog** directory of your **blog** application where all of our templates extend from and add the following code after the content block:

```
{% if messages %}
  {% for message in messages %}
    <div class="alert alert-{{ message.tags }} alert-dismissible fade show custom-alert" role="alert">
      <strong>{{ message }}</strong>
      <button type="button" class="close" data-dismiss="alert" aria-label="Close">
        <span aria-hidden="true">×</span>
      </button>
    </div>
  {% endfor %}
{% endif %}
```

Code 26 financeblog\blog\templates\blog\base.html

We are checking if any messages have been sent. If there are messages, we are looping over the sent messages and displaying them through the **message** variable inside an alert container. The color of the alert is determined by the **message.tags** variable, which will tell us the type of message i.e., success, info or warning etc. Next, we are displaying the actual message. After making the changes, your **base.html** file should look like this:

```
{% load static %}

<!doctype html>
<html lang="en">
  <head>
    <meta charset="utf-8">
    <meta name="viewport" content="width=device-width, initial-scale=1, shrink-to-fit=no">
    <link rel="stylesheet" href="https://cdn.jsdelivr.net/npm/bootstrap@4.5.3/dist/css/boo
tstrap.min.css" integrity="sha384-
TX8t27EcRE3e/ihU7zmQxVncDAy5uIKz4rEkgIXeMed4M0jlfIDPvg6uqKI2xXr2" crossorigin="anonymous">
    <link rel="preconnect" href="https://fonts.gstatic.com">
    <link href="https://fonts.googleapis.com/css2?family=Poppins:wght@400;600;700&display=
swap" rel="stylesheet">
    <link rel="stylesheet" type="text/css" href="{% static 'blog/main.css' %}">
    <title>My Finance Blog</title>
  </head>
  <body class="bg-light">
<header>
    <nav class="navbar navbar-expand-lg navbar-dark bg-dark">
        <div class="container">
          <a class="navbar-brand mb-
0 h1" href="{% url 'blog_list' %}">My Financial Blog</a>
        </div>
      </nav>
</header>

{% block content %}
{% endblock content %}
 {% if messages %}
  {% for message in messages %}
    <div class="alert alert-{{ message.tags }} alert-dismissible fade show custom-
alert" role="alert">
      <strong>{{ message }}</strong>
      <button type="button" class="close" data-dismiss="alert" aria-label="Close">
        <span aria-hidden="true">×</span>
      </button>
    </div>
  {% endfor %}
{% endif %}
    <script src="https://code.jquery.com/jquery-3.5.1.min.js" integrity="sha256-
9/aliU8dGd2tb6OSsuzixeV4y/faTqgFtohetphbbj0=" crossorigin="anonymous"></script>
    <script src="https://cdn.jsdelivr.net/npm/bootstrap@4.5.3/dist/js/bootstrap.bundle.min
.js" integrity="sha384-
ho+j7jyWK8fNQe+A12Hb8AhRq26LrZ/JpcUGGOn+Y7RsweNrtN/tE3MoK7ZeZDyx" crossorigin="anonymous">
</script>
    <script src="https://cdn.jsdelivr.net/npm/js-
cookie@rc/dist/js.cookie.min.js"></script>
  </body>
</html>
```

Code 27 financeblog\blog\templates\blog\base.html

Now go to http://localhost:8000/register and create a user. After you create the user and get redirected to the home page, you should now see an alert message in the right bottom corner.

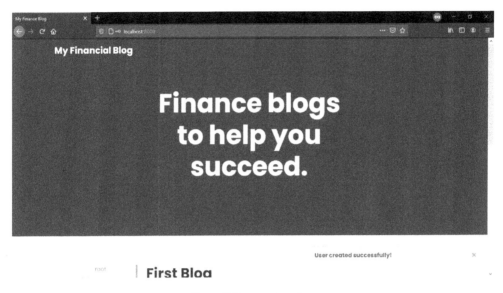

Figure 40 User creation alert

Remember the one-time message we talked about? Refresh the page, and you should not see the alert message again. This is very useful to notify the user whether an action took place and whether that action was successful or not.

LOGIN AND LOGOUT

CREATING VIEWS

Now that we have built the register view, it only makes sense to create the login and logout views. Django's built-in auth application already has a login and logout view, so we will use them instead of making ours from scratch.

By default, these views will render the admin site's template page, but we will be changing these defaults to display our custom templates. Open the **urls.py** file of the project inside the **financeblog** directory and add the following import:

```
from django.contrib.auth import views as auth_views
```

We are importing the views of Django's auth application as **auth_views**. Next, add the following URL patterns inside the URL patterns list.

```
path('login/', auth_views.LoginView.as_view(template_name="profiles/login.html"), name="lo
gin"),
path('logout/', auth_views.LogoutView.as_view(template_name="profiles/logout.html"), name=
"logout"),
```

We are creating two new URL patterns for login and logout. We are then using Django auth's **LoginView** and **LogoutView**. Note that these are class-based views (so far, we've only made functional views, but we will get into these shortly) and add class-based views.

We must add them by calling the function **as_view** of a class-based view. Next, you can see that we are passing a **template_name** to the **as_view** function. This will determine what template to display for these views. After making the changes, your project's **urls.py** file inside the **financeblog** directory should look like this.

```
from django.contrib import admin
from django.urls import path, include
from django.conf import settings
from django.conf.urls.static import static
from profiles import views as profiles_views
#NEW CODE BELOW
from django.contrib.auth import views as auth_views
#NEW CODE ABOVE
urlpatterns = [
    path('admin/', admin.site.urls),
    path('', include('blog.urls')),
    # user related paths below
    path('register/', profiles_views.register, name="register"),
    path('login/', auth_views.LoginView.as_view(template_name="profiles/login.html"), name
="login"),
    path('logout/', auth_views.LogoutView.as_view(template_name="profiles/logout.html"), n
ame="logout"),
    # user related paths above
]
urlpatterns += static(settings.MEDIA_URL, document_root=settings.MEDIA_ROOT)
```

Code 28 financeblog\financeblog\urls.py

By default, LoginView will redirect us to a path of "**accounts/profile**". We don't want that. We want to redirect to our homepage if a user logged in successfully. Open the **settings.py** file inside the **financeblog** directory and add the following setting.

```
LOGIN_REDIRECT_URL = "blog_list"
```

Upon successful login, this setting will redirect us to the"**blog_list**" URL, which is the name we gave to the homepage path.

CREATING TEMPLATES

We've defined the paths for the login and logout templates, but they don't exist yet. Create two files, **login.html** and **logout.html**, inside the **templates>profiles** directory of your **profiles** application. Your profiles application should now have the following directory structure for the **templates** directory.

Open the newly created **login.html** file and add the following code to it.

```
{% extends "blog/base.html" %}
{% load crispy_forms_tags %}
{% block content %}
<div class="landing bg-dark">
    <div class="container">
        <div class="row align-items-center justify-content-center">
            <div class="col-sm-12 col-lg-6 text-center">
                <h1 class="text-white font-weight-bold display-3 mb-3">Log In</h1>
            </div>
        </div>
    </div>
</div>
<div class="container bg-light mt-n5 p-5 rounded ">
    <div class="row">
        <div class="col-12">
            <form method="POST">
                {% csrf_token %}
                {{form|crispy}}
                <div class="form-group">
                    <button class="btn btn-outline-dark">Submit</button>
                </div>
                <a href="{% url 'register' %}">Register?</a>
                <a href="#">Forgot Password?</a>
            </form>
        </div>
    </div>
</div>
{% endblock content %}
```

Code 29 financeblog\profiles\templates\profiles\login.html

This template is no different from our **register.html** template other than the fact that the heading now says "Login" and we've added two links below the form. One link leads to the register page and the other link for "Forgot Password" currently leads you nowhere. Open the **logout.html** file we just created add the following code to it:

```
{% extends "blog/base.html" %}
{% block content %}
<div class="container bg-light mt-5 p-5 rounded ">
    <div class="row">
        <div class="col-12">
            <h2>You have been logged out.</h2>
            <a href="{% url 'blog_list' %}">Home</a>
        </div>
    </div>
</div>
{% endblock content %}
```

Code 30 financeblog\profiles\templates\profiles\logout.html

If we are logged in and visit the logout link, Django will log us out and show us this template. We are adding a link to the home page. Make sure you are logged out by visiting the admin site. Next, Open http://localhost:8000/login. I will intentionally enter incorrect credentials to see if we receive error messages as expected.

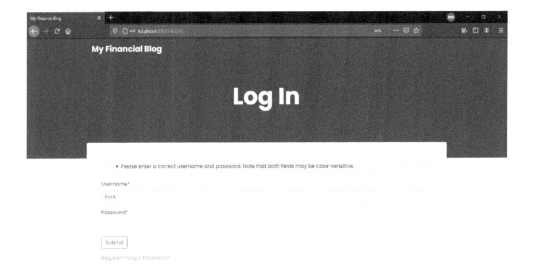

Figure 41 Login View

174

Django 3 for Beginners

You can see that it does work. Now log in with the superuser and visit the admin site. You should be logged in. Let's check our logout page. Make sure you are logged in and visit the link http://localhost:8000/logout.

You have been logged out.

Figure 42 After Successful login

Now visit the admin site to check if you were logged out, and if you are shown the login screen, it should mean that you were indeed logged out successfully. Now that we have created the login page, we should go to the register template and add the login page link. Open the **register.html** file and scroll down to where it says:

```
<a href="#">Login?</a>
```

Now change its href, so it points to our login page:

```
<a href="{% url 'login' %}">Login?</a>
```

GLOBAL NAVIGATION BAR

Currently, we have no way to differentiate whether a user is logged in or not. We have to check with the admin site every time - obviously not usable. Let's display the **login** and **register** links in the Navigation Bar if the user is not logged in and show a **logout** link if the user is logged in.

Open the **base.html** file inside the **blog** application's **templates > blog** directory. Replace the **header** html tag with the following code.

```
<header>
  <nav class="navbar navbar-expand-lg navbar-dark bg-dark">
    <div class="container">
      <a class="navbar-brand mb-0 h1" href="{% url 'blog_list' %}">My Financial Blog</a>
      <button class="navbar-toggler" type="button" data-toggle="collapse" data-
target="#navbarSupportedContent"
        aria-controls="navbarSupportedContent" aria-expanded="false" aria-label="Toggle
navigation">
        <span class="navbar-toggler-icon"></span>
      </button>
      <div class="collapse navbar-collapse" id="navbarSupportedContent">
        <ul class="navbar-nav ml-auto">
          {% if request.user.is_authenticated %}

          <li class="nav-item">
            <a href="#" class="nav-link">Profile</a>
          </li>
          <li class="nav-item">
            <a href="{% url 'logout' %}" class="nav-link">Logout</a>
          </li>
          {% else %}
          <li class="nav-item">
            <a href="{% url 'login' %}" class="nav-link">Login</a>
          </li>
          <li class="nav-item">
            <a href="{% url 'register' %}" class="nav-link">Register</a>
          </li>
          {% endif %}
        </ul>
      </div>
    </div>
  </nav>
</header>
```

Code 31 financeblog\blog\templates\blog\base.html

Using the **request** object, we have access to the **user** object associated with a **request**. We are creating navigation links and we have added a conditional using the **if** template tag.

We are using the attribute **is_authenticated** to determine whether the user is logged in or not. This value will be **False** if we are logged out and **True** when we are logged in. If we are authenticated, we are showing two links, **logout** and **profile.**

The profile doesn't lead us anywhere currently and the logout page direct us to the logout page. If we are not authenticated, We are displaying the login and register navigations links. Remember that we are building the urls using the **url** template tag and passing it the name we gave our URL patterns. Guests will see the following navigation bar.

Figure 43 After logout

When you are logged in, you should see Profiles and Logout:

Figure 44 Logged In. Hence there is a logout option

CREATING PROFILE FRONTEND

PROFILE VIEW

Let's create a profile view that will be responsible for displaying the profile of a user. Open the **views.py** of the **profiles** application and add the following view.

```
def profile(request, pk):
    user = get_object_or_404(User, pk=pk)
    return render(request, "profiles/profile.html", {"user": user})
```

Code 32 financeblog\profiles\views.py

This value is the same as our blog detail view. The only difference is we are fetching a User. It will display a 404 error if no user is found matching the **pk** we provide our view. Make sure to import the **get_object_or_404** function and **User** model.

Warning, this file is missing two imports, and you need to figure out what is missing and import it (If you need help, take a look at it).

PROFILE URLS

Open the **urls.py** file of the project inside the **financeblog** directory and add the following URL pattern to the **urlpatterns** list:

```
path('profile/<int:pk>',profiles_views.profile,name="profile")
```

Code 33 financeblog\blog\urls.py

This URL pattern is also very similar to our blog detail view's URL pattern. We are passing a value pk of type int, which means it will be a number. Next, we are routing the **profile** view we created in our views file to the pattern. We're also giving this URL pattern a name of a profile.

PROFILE TEMPLATE

You know by now, add a file called **profile.html** inside the **templates>profiles** directory of your **profiles** application, where all of our **profiles** application's templates live. Add the following markup to it:

```
{% extends "blog/base.html" %}
{% block content %}
<div class="container">
    <div class="row pt-5">
        <div class="col-sm-12 col-lg-3 mb-3 text-center">
            <img class="profile-image" src="{{ user.profile.image.url }}" alt="Hello">
        </div>
        <div class="col-sm-12 col-lg-9">
            <h1 class="font-weight-bold">{{user.first_name}} {{user.last_name}}</h1>
            <p>{{user.profile.description}}</p>
            {% if request.user ==  user %}
                <div class="links">
                    <a href="#" class="btn btn-sm btn-primary">Update Profile</a>
                </div>
            {% endif %}
        </div>
    </div>
</div>
{% endblock content %}
```

Code 34 financeblog/profiles/templates/profiles/profiles.html

As always, we are extending from the **base.html** template. We are displaying the user's first name and last name. Next, we are showing the description field that we added to the profile model.

Note that the User model and the Profile model share a one-to-one relationship. So we can reverse-lookup the profile associated with a user using the **user.profile.some_field** syntax. That is how we are accessing the description field on the profile of a specific user.

We are displaying the image we added to the profile model. We are accessing the image's URL that is available by the URL value we have available on image fields. If the user uploaded an image, it would show that one, and if they didn't, it would show the default one.

Before we move any further, let's add our profile page link to the navigation bar. Currently, there is a link on the navigation bar shown to logged-in users called profile, but it doesn't take you anywhere. Open the **base.html** file inside the blog application's template folder and find the navigation tag:

```
<li class="nav-item">
    <a href="#" class="nav-link">Profile</a>
</li>
```

Code 35 financeblog\blog\templates\blog\base.html

Now change it's href so it leads us to our logged in user's profile:

```
<li class="nav-item">
    <a href="{% url 'profile' request.user.pk %}" class="nav-link">Profile</a>
</li>
```

Code 36 financeblog\blog\templates\blog\base.html

We are passing it the **profile** url and also passing it the current logged in user's pk that is available to us on the request object. Now open the development server and visit the site. Make sure you are logged in and open; click on the **profile** link in the navigation bar. It should lead you to the profile page of the logged-in user:

Figure 45 Logged In user

You can see that it works perfectly. Note that you can access other user's profiles as well by directly typing their URL address. For example, this is the profile of another user:

Figure 46 Different user profile

Right away, you can notice that this user is not showing the "**update profile**" button. This is because of the conditional "**{% if request.user == user %}**" in the template. We are checking if the user viewing the page (request.user) is the same user we are displaying (user).

This means users will only be shown the update button on their profile page only when they are logged in. Currently, this button leads you nowhere as we haven't added a profile update view yet.

You should also notice that this user has no description yet, and that is because it is blank. On our register page, we were only accepting User model information. We need a form to fill the description field or a default description provider.

We never showed the description and image fields of the Profile model to the user. That was to keep the view simple and not overload the form. We will now also add the field image and description of the profile model on our update page. So our users can edit the details of their page once they've signed up.

PROFILE UPDATE FORMS

Remember that User and Profile are two separate models. That is why we will create two forms that extend from **ModelForm** class. Open the **forms.py** file of the **profiles** application and add the following two forms:

```
class UserUpdateForm(forms.ModelForm):
    email = forms.EmailField(required=True)
    first_name = forms.CharField(max_length=50, required=True)
    last_name = forms.CharField(max_length=50, required=True)
    class Meta:
        model = User
        fields = [ 'email', 'username', 'first_name', 'last_name']
class ProfileUpdateForm(forms.ModelForm):
    description = forms.CharField(widget=forms.Textarea, max_length=500, required=False)

    class Meta:
        model = Profile
        fields = ['description', 'image']
```

Figure 47 finanaceblog/profiles/forms.py

By the way, one import is missing in the code above...will you figure it out before getting an Exception? We are creating two forms. Let's look at **UserUpdateForm**. It is very similar to our RegisterForm, but it is different as it doesn't extend from **UserCreationForm**. We are only updating the user and not creating it. That's why we will not be using the register form.

We are redefining the email, first_name, and last_name fields to make them required. Next, under the Meta class, we tell that we want this form tied to the User model. As for the fields, we are not including the password fields as we will not be updating those on the update page.

In the **ProfileUpdateForm**, we are redefining the description field. We set the description as a CharField on the model definitions. By default, Django forms will render CharField as HTML input of type text. However, we want to show this field as an HTML textarea. We can do that through the **widgets** attribute of a form field. That is why we are redefining the description field in the **ProfileUpdateForm.**

We are also giving it a limit of 500 characters and setting the required attribute to False. Next, under the metaclass, we are setting the Profile model to this form. We are then assigning the image and description values to the fields variable inside the Meta class. Our form will automatically generate the input for the image field.

PROFILE UPDATE VIEW

Open the **views.py** inside the **profiles** application and add the following imports:

```
from django.contrib.auth.decorators import login_required
from .forms import UserUpdateForm, ProfileUpdateForm
```

Code 37 financeblog\profiles\views.py

Next, add the following code to create the profile update view:

```
@login_required
def update(request):
    if request.POST:
        user_form = UserUpdateForm(request.POST, instance=request.user)
        profile_form = ProfileUpdateForm(request.POST, request.FILES, instance=request.use
r.profile)
        if user_form and profile_form:
            user_form.save()
            profile_form.save()
            messages.success(request, "Profile Updated Successfully!")
            return redirect('profile', request.user.pk)
    else:
        user_form = UserUpdateForm(instance=request.user)
        profile_form = ProfileUpdateForm(instance=request.user.profile)
    context = {
        'user_form': user_form,
        'profile_form': profile_form,
    }
    return render(request, 'profiles/update.html', context)
```

Code 38 financeblog\profiles\views.py

We are wrapping our update view with the **login_required** decorator function we imported. It will only allow logged-in users to access this page. Next, as we did in the register view, we are checking if the request is of type POST or not. If it is, we are creating instances of the **UserUpdateForm** and **ProfileUpdateForm** and passing them the user-submitted data through the request.POST and request.FILES. Any

186

images or files the user sends through the form are not available under **request.POST**, but somewhat under **request.FILES**. That is why we are passing it to our **ProfileUpdateForm** along with the request.POST.

We are also passing the forms an **instance** parameter. To the **UserUpdateForm,** we are passing the currently logged-in user available under **request.user** and to the **ProfileUpdateForm** we are passing the profile of the current user available under **request.user.profile**. This will tell the form to update these instances and not create new instances of the models on calling the save method.

Then we are calling the **is_valid** method on both of the forms. If both of the forms were validated, we are calling the save method on the form. This will update the instances of the user and profile model. If the forms were not valid, it will send us back to the update page with errors. After the form is saved we are creating a flash message and redirecting the user back to the profile page.

If the request method was not POST, it means the user opened the update page. We are, again, instantiating both of the forms, but this time we aren't passing the request.POST or request.FILES as no POST request was made. We are still passing the instances to the form to make sure our form fields are pre-populated so the user is not shown a blank form.

We are creating a dictionary by the name of context and assigning it our forms under keys of "user_form" and "profile_form". Lastly, we are returning the render method with the path of the template and context.

The last thing we need to do is set our **LOGIN_REDIRECT** setting. Our **login_required** needs to know where to redirect unauthenticated users. Open the **setttings.py** file inside the **financeblog** directory and add the following setting:

```
LOGIN_URL = "login"
```

The name **"login"** here is the name we gave our login path. It will redirect logged-out users if they try accessing this page.

PROFILE UPDATE URL

Add the following URL pattern to the urlpatterns list inside the **urls.py** inside the **financeblog** directory:

```
path('profile/update', profiles_views.update, name="update"),
```

Code 39 financeblog\blog\urls.py

Our updated view will now be available under the 'profile/update' path. We gave it the name "update".

PROFILE UPDATE TEMPLATE

Create a file called **update.html** inside the **templates>profiles** directory of the **profiles** application and add:

```
{% extends "blog/base.html" %}
{% load crispy_forms_tags %}
{% block content %}
<div class="landing bg-dark">
    <div class="container">
        <div class="row align-items-center justify-content-center">
            <div class="col-sm-12 col-lg-6 text-center">
                <h1 class="text-white font-weight-bold display-3 mb-3">Update</h1>
            </div>
        </div>
    </div>
</div>
<div class="container bg-light mt-n5 p-5 rounded blog">
    <div class="row">
        <div class="col-12">
            <form method="POST" enctype="multipart/form-data">
                {% csrf_token %}
                {{user_form|crispy}}
                {{profile_form|crispy}}
                <div class="form-group">
                    <button class="btn btn-outline-dark">Submit</button>
                </div>
            </form>
        </div>
    </div>
</div>
{% endblock content %}
```

Code 40 finanaceblog/profiles/templates/profiles/update.py

Everything is the same as our previous templates. The only thing different is that now we are displaying two forms. It is excellent to display more than one Django form inside a single page. Note that our HTML form also has an **enctype** property. This is compulsory when sending files over the form. If we don't specify this, our image will not be sent to the view.

Before checking the form, let's quickly link it inside the profile page. If you remember, the "Update Profile" link is currently dead. Open the **profile.html** file inside the **templates>profiles** directory of the **profiles** application and find this link:

```
<a href="#" class="btn btn-sm btn-primary">Update Profile</a>
```

Change it to the following, so it leads the user to the profile update page:

```
<a href="{% url 'update' %}" class="btn btn-sm btn-primary">Update Profile</a>
```

Now, if you open http://localhost:8000/profile/update and you should see the following.

Figure 48 Update form

You can see all the fields are pre-populated. You can also see that both the user and the profile forms are showing just fine. Upon updating some fields and saving the form, you should be redirected to this page:

Figure 49 Profile Update Notification

PASSWORD RESET

Our **profiles** application is almost complete. The only thing left is to create a password reset functionality so users can reset their password if they forget it. We will send the users an email that will contain a link, using which they will reset their passwords.

SETTING UP SMTP HOST

To send mails, we have to set up an SMTP host. We will use our Gmail account to send emails but note that this is not suitable for a production environment.

To send mails from Gmail, you have to allow a less secure app access to your Gmail. To do this, make sure you are logged in to your Google account and visit https://myaccount.google.com.

Click the **Security** setting on the left sidebar and scroll down to where it says "Less secure app access" and turn it on.

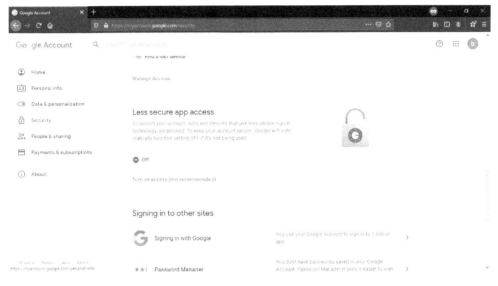

Figure 50 Google Security

If you have 2-step-auth activated, you need to create a new "App Password" and use this password instead of your actual google password. It's advised to delete the App Password after the development is finished.

Now open the **settings.py** file of your project and add the following settings to it:

```
EMAIL_BACKEND = 'django.core.mail.backends.smtp.EmailBackend'
EMAIL_HOST = 'smtp.gmail.com'
EMAIL_PORT = 587
EMAIL_USE_TLS = True
EMAIL_HOST_USER=''
EMAIL_HOST_PASSWORD=''
```

Code 41 financeblog\financeblog\settings.py

Let's go over these fields:

- **EMAIL_BACKEND**: Through this setting, we are telling that we want to use send mails over SMTP. There are other options available such as a console backend or file backend.
- **EMAIL_HOST:** This setting takes the host of our SMTP. We are using Gmail.
- **EMAIL_PORT:** This is the port to use for the SMTP server.
- **EMAIL_USE_TLS:** This determines whether to use a secure connection when communicating with the SMTP server.
- **EMAIL_HOST_USER:** This field will hold our Gmail email account.
- **EMAIL_HOST_PASSWORD:** This field will hold the password for the Gmail account.

In simple terms, using these settings, we are telling Django that we will be sending our mail through a Gmail account.

In the EMAIL_HOST_USER and EMAIL_HOST_PASSWORD settings, you must add your Gmail account's email and password as strings. These will settings will use your Gmail account to send mails. I've added my credentials to the **EMAIL_HOST_USER** and **EMAIL_HOST_PASSWORD**, but I'm not showing them here for obvious security reasons. We are ready to create the reset password view for our profiles application.

PASSWORD RESET VIEWS

Django's auth application has a password reset feature already built for us. This feature uses 4 different views for the whole process. Open the **urls.py** file of the project, inside the **financeblog** directory and add the following URL patterns:

```
path('password-
reset/', auth_views.PasswordResetView.as_view(template_name="profiles/password_reset.html"
), name="password_reset"),
path('password-
reset/confirm/<uidb64>/<token>', auth_views.PasswordResetConfirmView.as_view(template_name
="profiles/password_reset_confirm.html"), name="password_reset_confirm"),
path('password-
reset/done', auth_views.PasswordResetDoneView.as_view(template_name="profiles/password_res
et_done.html"), name="password_reset_done"),
path('password-
reset/complete', auth_views.PasswordResetCompleteView.as_view(template_name="profiles/pass
word_reset_complete.html"), name="password_reset_complete"),
```

Code 42 financeblog\financeblog\urls.py

The first url pattern takes the view **PasswordResetView**. It will show us a form where we can submit our email address. It will then send a one-time password reset link to our email and redirect us to another view that will show a success note. Note that it will not alert us in case the entered email does not exist in our system.

The second URL pattern takes the view **PasswordResetConfrm**. This is the view that will actually allow us to change our password. The one-time link that is generated in the **PasswordResetView** is done through this view. It takes the user id encoded in base 64 and a token as its URL parameters.

The third URL pattern takes the view **PasswordResetDone**. This is the view that will be shown to the user once they submit their email on the **PasswordResetView,** and this view will only display a success message.

The fourth and last URL pattern takes the view **PasswordResetComplete**. After the user successfully changes their password, they are redirected to this page.

PASSWORD RESET TEMPLATES

Create 4 files, password_reset.html, password_reset_confirm.html, password_reset_done.html, password_reset_complete.html, and place them inside the templates>profiles directory of the profiles application.

Our templates directory has now the following directory structure.

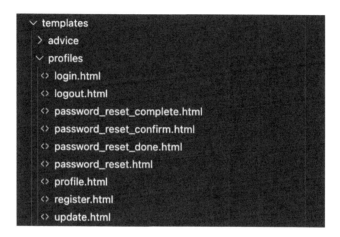

Open **password_reset.html** and add the following markup:

```
{% extends "blog/base.html" %}
{% load crispy_forms_tags %}
{% block content %}
<div class="landing bg-dark">
    <div class="container">
        <div class="row align-items-center justify-content-center">
            <div class="col-sm-12 col-lg-6 text-center">
                <h1 class="text-white font-weight-bold display-3 mb-3">Password Reset</h1>
            </div>
        </div>
    </div>
</div>
<div class="container bg-light mt-n5 p-5 rounded ">
    <div class="row">
        <div class="col-12">
            <form method="POST">
                {% csrf_token %}
                {{form|crispy}}
                <div class="form-group">
                    <button class="btn btn-outline-dark">Submit</button>
                </div>
            </form>
        </div>
    </div>
</div>
{% endblock content %}
```

Code 43 financeblog\profiles\templates\profiles\password_reset.html

It is the same as our other templates that display a form. We are displaying the heading "Password Reset". Next, we are displaying the form. In **password_reset_done.html**, add.

196

```
{% extends "blog/base.html" %}
{% block content %}
<div class="container bg-light mt-5 p-5 rounded ">
    <div class="row">
        <div class="col-12">
            <div class="alert alert-info">
                An email has been sent to you. Click the link in it to reset the password.
            </div>
        </div>
    </div>
</div>
{% endblock content %}
```

Code 44 financeblog\profiles\templates\profiles\password_reset_done.html

This template only displays a message to the user that they should check their email. It will be displayed once they have submitted the password reset form. In **password_reset_confirm.html**, add:

```
{% extends "blog/base.html" %}
{% load crispy_forms_tags %}
{% block content %}
<div class="landing bg-dark">
    <div class="container">
        <div class="row align-items-center justify-content-center">
            <div class="col-sm-12 col-lg-6 text-center">
                <h1 class="text-white font-weight-bold display-3 mb-
3">Password Confirm?</h1>
            </div>
        </div>
    </div>
</div>
<div class="container bg-light mt-n5 p-5 rounded ">
    <div class="row">
        <div class="col-12">
            <form method="POST">
                {% csrf_token %}
                {{form|crispy}}
                <div class="form-group">
                    <button class="btn btn-outline-dark">Reset Password</button>
                </div>
            </form>
        </div>
    </div>
</div>
{% endblock content %}
```

Code 45 financeblog\profiles\templates\profiles\password_reset_confirm.html

This template, again, is the same as our **password_reset.html** template. Users will
be taken to this template when they click on the link they receive in the password
reset email. In **password_reset_complete.html**, add.

```
{% extends "blog/base.html" %}
{% block content %}
<div class="container bg-light mt-5 p-5 rounded ">
    <div class="row">
        <div class="col-12">
            <div class="alert alert-success">
                Password Reset Successful!
            </div>
            <a href="{% url 'login' %}">Log in?</a>
        </div>
    </div>
</div>
{% endblock content %}
```

Code 46 financeblog\profiles\templates\profiles\password_reset_complete.html

In this template, we are displaying that the user was able to reset the password successfully. We are also adding a link to our **login** page.

Speaking of which, currently, there is a "**Forgot Password?**" link on our login page that currently leads you nowhere. Let's edit that so it leads you to the password reset page. Open the **login.html** file inside **tempates>profiles** directory of the profiles application and find the following line:

```
<a href="#">Forgot Password?</a>
```

Change the href so it points to our password reset view:

```
<a href="{% url 'password_reset' %}">Forgot Password?</a>
```

TESTING PASSWORD RESET

Let's test the password reset feature. Make sure you are logged out and visit http://localhost:8000/password_reset:

Figure 51 Password Reset form

It works. Enter the email of the user, and it should lead you to the following page:

Figure 52 Password reset email sent

Django 3 for Beginners

Now open your inbox. You should have received an email from the Gmail account you used for the SMTP server:

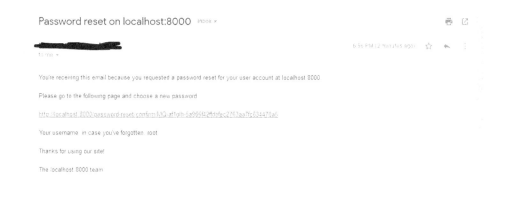

Figure 53 Password reset email

I've received the mail. On clicking the link inside the mail, it should lead me to the following page:

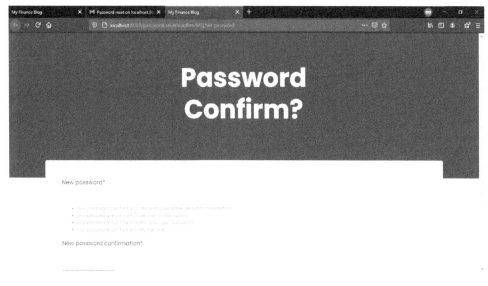

Figure 54 New Password form

This is the page where we will reset the password. Change the password, and you'll see that our password reset feature is working correctly. And the best part is that we didn't even have to create it ourselves. We just hooked it into our project and provided our custom templates for it.

VIEWS

Now that we have a working user system on our website where users can register, login, log out, reset the password, etc. We should now consider adding more features to our blog application. We will now add **create**, **update** and **delete** views for the blog application, and we will make these using class-based views.

In the above figure, we can see that we have completed the up-to user authentication part in our blog application. And we will currently do the other parts.

GENERIC CLASS BASED VIEWS

INTRODUCTION

So far, we've only created functional views. Django also has class-based views. We can use either classes or functions to build our views.

Django also has **generic** class-based views. In simple terms, these are views that allow us to do everyday web development tasks with very little code as possible. Several generic class-based views are available to us, such as CreateView, which allows us to create a "create" view for a model quickly without creating a form. There is also a ListView which allows us to list objects of a model very quickly. Let's use these generic class-based views and learn how not to code too much.

TEMPLATE NAMING CONVENTION

By default, Django's generic views look for templates under the path **"(application)/(model)_(viewtype).html"** where **application** refers to the name of the application, **model** refers to the name of the model we passed our generic view, and **viewtype** refers to the type of generic view we are creating.

However, views created from the **CreateView, UpdateView,** and **DeleteView** generic views are an exception to this naming convention.

CreateView and **UpdateVIew** will share the same template, and the template name is "**(model)_form**.html". The "**model**" here is the name of the model. We will pass the generic view, but the "form" after the underscore character is literal. **DeleteView** template name is "**(model)_confirm_delete**". Model refers to the name of the model, and "_confirm_delete" are literal.

We can change these defaults by the **tempate_name** attribute on the view. However, we will go with the default template naming convention.

BLOG CREATE VIEW

BASIC USE CASE OF GENERIC VIEWS

Let's create a **BlogCreateView** using the generic **CreateView**. Open the **views.py** file of the **blog** application and add the following import:

```
from django.views import generic
```

Code 47 financeblog\blog\views.py

Next add the following code:

```
class BlogCreateView(generic.CreateView):
    model = Blog
    fields = ['title', 'content']
    def form_valid(self, form):
        form.instance.author = self.request.user
        return super().form_valid(form)
```

Code 48 financeblog\blog\views.py

We are creating a class-based view that extends from the generic **CreateView** class. It will allow us to create a "Create" view very quickly without writing a form.

A view that inherits from **CreateView** has two required attributes, i.e., **model** and **fields**. For the model, we are assigning it Blog, and for fields, we are assigning it the **title** and **content.** Note that we left out the **date_published** field as it will automatically get added according to the model definitions. We are also not passing the **author** field because we want to set the currently logged-in user as the author of the blog automatically.

Next, we are overriding the **form_valid** method and setting the currently logged-in user (available inside the request object) as the author for the blog we are creating.

We are doing it this way because currently, the author is unset as we didn't pass it through the **fields** attribute. We didn't pass the author through the fields attribute because it will then show the user a dropdown of users to select from like it does in the admin site. We obviously don't want that and want to associate the current logged-in user with the author of the blog.

Currently, anybody can access this view whether they are logged in or not. We also have no way to send a flash message when the blog is created. We can't use the messages function or the **login_required** decorators as they are not suited for class-based views.

EXTENDING GENERIC VIEW

We will use the **LoginRequiredMixin** and **SuccessMessageMixin** mixin to fix this. Mixins are used to add additional functionalities to our class-based views. Let's import these at the top of the views.py file.

```
from django.contrib.auth.mixins import LoginRequiredMixin
from django.contrib.messages.views import SuccessMessageMixin
```

Code 49 financeblog\blog\views.py

Change the **CreateBlogView,** so it uses these mixins:

```
class BlogCreateView(LoginRequiredMixin, SuccessMessageMixin, generic.CreateView):
    model = Blog
    fields = ['title', 'content']
    success_message = "Blog Created Successfully!"

    def form_valid(self, form):
        form.instance.author = self.request.user
        return super().form_valid(form)
```

Code 50 financeblog\blog\views.py

Our **BlogCreateView** is now inheriting from the mixins we imported along with the **CreateView**. This is how you add mixins to class-based view, i.e. make your class inherit from them. We have also added a new attribute called **success_message,** which is the value that will be used to create the flash message when the blog is created successfully.

Let's add this view to the **urls.py** file of the **blog** application. Add the following URL pattern to the **urlpatterns** list:

```
path("blog/create", views.BlogCreateView.as_view(), name="blog_create")
```

206

This view will be available to use under the path "blog/create". Since we can't just pass a class to a URL pattern, we pass **BlogCreateView** view by calling its **as_view** method.

Now we should add the template for this view. According to the template naming convention of generic views we discussed previously, our **BlogCreateVIew** will look for its template under "**blog/blog_form.html**". Once again, this can be overridden, but we will stick with the naming convention. Next, create a file called **blog_form.html** that is in the **templates>blog** directory of the blog application. Add the following code to it:

```
{% extends "blog/base.html" %}
{% load crispy_forms_tags %}
{% block content %}
<div class="landing bg-dark">
    <div class="container">
        <div class="row align-items-center justify-content-center">
            <div class="col-sm-12 col-lg-6 text-center">
                <h1 class="text-white font-weight-bold display-3 mb-3">Blog</h1>
            </div>
        </div>
    </div>
</div>
<div class="container bg-light mt-n5 p-5 rounded ">
    <div class="row">
        <div class="col-12">
            <form method="POST">
                {% csrf_token %}
                {{form|crispy}}
                <div class="form-group">
                    <button class="btn btn-outline-dark">Submit</button>
                </div>
            </form>
        </div>
    </div>
</div>
{% endblock content %}
```

Code 52 financeblog\blog\templates\blog\blog_form.html

It is a simple form template, very similar to the templates we've created so far. The CreateView and UpdateView send their form under the **form** variable to the template. It's great that we didn't even have to create a form ourselves as the **CreateView** takes care of it for us.

Let's test it out. First, make sure you are logged out and open http://localhost:8000/blog/create. It should redirect you to the login page. Now login and open the page again:

Figure 55 Blog Create View

It is only displaying the **title** and the **content** fields as we set in the view. When we submit the form, it will set the currently logged-in user as the author of this blog because of the form_valid method overriding. Let's fill the form to create a blog:

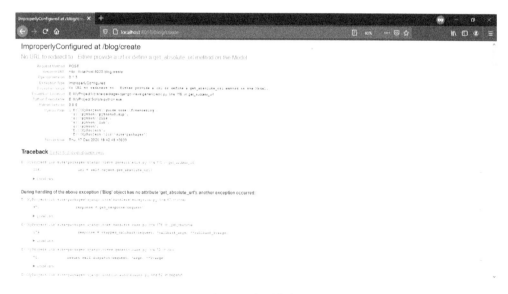

Figure 56 Blog filled up

It will show you this error page. Don't worry, and our blog was created just fine. Reading the error reveals the message "No URL to redirect to. Either provide a URL or define a get_absolute_url method on the Model.".

The generic CreateView will try to redirect us to the newly created model instance on success, but it doesn't know it's URL path. It will look for a method called **get_absolute_url** on the model, which will generate a URL for the detailed view of the newly created instance. This method, by convention in Django, is used to create URLs for instances of models.

Let's create the get_absolute_url method on our **Blog** model. Open the **models.py** file of the blog application and add the following import:

```
from django.urls import reverse
```

Next, add the following method to the **Blog** model class:

```
def get_absolute_url(self):
    return reverse("blogs_detail", kwargs={'pk': self.pk})
```

Code 53 financeblog\blog\models.py

The **reverse** function takes a URL and additional keyword arguments. If you remember, **blogs_detail** is the name of our **detail_blog** view, which displays the blog's detail page, and it takes a **pk** parameter. We are passing the current blog instance's pk as the pk parameter to the URL. Lastly, the reverse function will generate a URL and return it.

Let's test the create view again. Create a view, and now it should lead you to its detail page:

Figure 57 Detailed View

Figure 58 Successful redirection on the detailed view

Django successfully redirected us to the detail page of the newly created blog. It also shows our flash message.

BLOG UPDATE VIEW

Let's create an **update** view of our blog. We only want the author of the blog to be able to update it. Any user that tries to access the update page of a blog they are not the author of will be shown a "**Forbidden**" page (HTTP Status: 403).

Add the import to the **views.py** file of the blog application:

```
from django.contrib.auth.mixins import UserPassesTestMixin
```

Add the following code to create the update view for our blog:

```
class BlogUpdateView(LoginRequiredMixin, UserPassesTestMixin, SuccessMessageMixin, generic
.UpdateView):
    model = Blog
    fields = ['title', 'content']
    success_message = "Blog Updated Successfully!"

    def form_valid(self, form):
        form.instance.author = self.request.user
        return super().form_valid(form)

    def test_func(self):
        blog = self.get_object()
        if self.request.user == blog.author:
            return True
        else:
            return False
```

Code 54 financeblog\blog\views.py

This view is the same as our **BlogCreateView** except for three changes. First, it inherits from **UpdateView** instead of **CreateView**. The difference between the two is that the **UpdateView** will be expecting a **pk** parameter in its **URL** pattern for identifying a model instance that we will be changing. It will be updating an instance instead of creating a new one.

The second change is that we are now adding another mixin, **UserPassesTestMixin**, to our update view. Using this mixin, we can add a conditional pass to only allow access to this view if the currently logged-in user is the author of this blog.

Third and last change is the **test_func** method. This method is where you put the conditional pass for the **UserPassesTestMixin**. In it, we are first fetching the current blog that we are updating. Next, we are checking whether the current user is the author of the blog. If our current user is the author, we return True to indicate that it is okay to allow access, else it will restrict access.

Let's add the URL pattern for this view. Open the **urls.py** file of the **blog** application and add the following URL pattern to the URL pattern list:

```
path('blog/<int:pk>/update', views.BlogUpdateView.as_view(), name="blog_update")
```

UpdateView requires a **pk** parameter in the URL pattern, and we are passing that. We have given our blog update view the name **blog_update**.

Both the **CreateView** and **UpdateView** generic views use the same template, so we don't have to create a template for our **BlogUpdateView** as it will use the template for the **BlogCreateView**.

Now to test it out, visit http://localhost:8000/blog/6/update. Note that "6" here is the pk of one of my blogs. If you enter a random pk in the URL and no blog exists matching that pk, it will show a 404 error.

Figure 59 Blog Updating

Figure 60 Blog Update successful

You can see that it showed us the form, and it was prepopulated with our existing data. The flash message is also saying that it was updated successfully

BLOG DELETE

GENERIC DELETE VIEW

Users should be able to delete their blogs. Let's add a delete view. Open the **views.py** file of the blog application and add the following code:

```python
class BlogDeleteView(LoginRequiredMixin, UserPassesTestMixin, generic.DeleteView):
    model = Blog
    success_message  = "Blog Deleted Successfully!"
    success_url = "/"

    def test_func(self):
        blog = self.get_object()
        if self.request.user == blog.author:
            return True
        else:
            return False

    def delete(self, request, *args, **kwargs):
        messages.success(self.request, self.success_message)
        return super(BlogDeleteView, self).delete(request, *args, **kwargs)
```

Code 55 financeblog\blog\views.py

Our **BlogDeleteView** extends from the generic **DeleteView**. The only required value for views that extend from **DeleteView** is the model attribute. We are ensuring that only the author of the blog can delete the blog through the **UserPassesTestMixin**.

If you noticed, we are not using the **SuccessMessageMixin** in our **BlogDeleteView**. The **SuccessMessageMixin** works by hooking itself on the **form_valid,** but the **form_valid** method is not present in the generic **DeleteVIew,** so it will not work.

That is why we are overriding **BlogDeleteView**'s **delete** method and sending a flash message of type success. We are passing it **self.success_message,** which refers to the **success_message** attribute we created on **BlogDetailView** class. Note that we are only overriding the **delete** method because we want to show a flash message. This is not required by the **DeleteView**. Since we are using the **messages** object, make sure you don't forget to import it:

```
from django.contrib import messages
```

Let's add **BlogDeleteView**'s URL pattern. Open the **urls.py** file of the blog application and add the following URL pattern to the urlpatterns list:

```
path('blog/<int:pk>/delete', views.BlogDeleteView.as_view(), name="blog_delete"),
```

DELETE CONFIRMATION TEMPLATE

As per the template naming convention we discussed earlier, it will look for a file called **blog_confirm_delete.html** as it's template. Open the **templates>blogs** directory of the **blog** application and create a file called **blog_confirm_delete.html**. Add the following content to it:

```
{% extends "blog/base.html" %}
{% load crispy_forms_tags %}
{% block content %}
<div class="container bg-light p-5 mt-5 rounded ">
    <div class="row">
        <div class="col-12">
            <h2>Are you sure you want to delete the blog "<strong>{{object.title}}</strong>"
?</h2>
                <form method="POST">
                    {% csrf_token %}
                    <div class="form-group">
                        <button class="btn btn-danger">Yes please.</button>
                        <a class="btn btn-
info" href="{% url 'blog_detail' object.pk %}">No, take me back</a>
                    </div>
                </form>
        </div>
    </div>
</div>
{% endblock content %}
```

Code 56 financeblog\blog\templates\blog\blog_confirm_delete.html

BlogDeleteView view will display a confirmation page on a GET request, i.e. opening the delete page. It will only delete the instance if we perform a POST request against it.

216

We are sending an empty form with only the **csrf_token** template tag. If we press the "Yes please." button, it will perform a POST request on the same URL, and our **BlogDeleteView** will then delete the blog instance. Let's delete a view to test it out. Open http://localhost:8000/blog/6/delete:

Figure 61 Deleting The blog

BLOG LIST VIEW

GENERIC LIST VIEW

Currently, we have the view **list_blogs** in the **blog** application that lists all the available blogs. We will use the generic **ListView** to do this instead. Open the **views.py** file of the **blog** application and remove the existing **list_blogs** and replace it with the following view:

```
class BlogListView(generic.ListView):
    model = Blog
    ordering = ['-date_published']
    paginate_by = 3
```

Code 57 financeblog\blog\views.py

We are creating a **BlogListView** view that extends from the generic **ListView**. The only required attribute for the **ListView** is the **model**. We have added an **ordering** attribute to order the queryset of blogs by the most recent blog created through the **date_published** field. Next, we are adding an attribute called **paginate_by**. This will add pagination to our view and will only show up to 3 blogs at a time. Also, note that we aren't using any mixins as we want all users to view the home page where we will list all the blogs.

Remember, just updating the view in views.py is not enough. We need to tell the "dispatcher" where to find the new view (and remove the pointer to the old view). Let's add this generic view to the **urls.py** file of our **blog** application. Find the following URL pattern, which currently uses our old **list_blog** view:

```
path("", views.list_blogs, name="blog_list"),
```

Change it to use our new **BlogListView:**

```
path("", views.BlogListView.as_view(), name="blog_list")
```

LIST VIEW TEMPLATE

Keeping the naming convention of generic views we discussed earlier in mind, and our **BlogListVIew** will look for its template under "**blog/blog_list.html**".

Now remove the existing **list.html** template in the **templates>blog** directory of the blog application and create **blog_list.html** file. Add the following code to it:

```html
{% extends "blog/base.html" %}
{% block content %}
<div class="landing bg-dark">
  <div class="container">
    <div class="row align-items-center justify-content-center">
      <div class="col-sm-12 col-lg-6 text-center">
        <h1 class="text-white font-weight-bold display-3 mb-3">Finance blogs to help you
succeed.</h1>
      </div>
    </div>
  </div>
</div>
<div class="container p-5 rounded ">
  {% if object_list.count > 0 %}
  {% for blog in object_list %}
  <div class="row blog mb-5">
    <div class="col-lg-2 col-sm-12 text-center">
      <a class="mugshot-container mb-1" href="{% url 'profile' blog.author.pk %}">
        <div class="mugshot-img mb-2" style="background-
image:url({{blog.author.profile.image.url}})"></div>
        <span>{{blog.author.username}}</span>
      </a>
      <small class="text-muted">{{blog.date_published|date:"d/m/Y h:i a"}}</small>
    </div>
    <div class="col-lg-10 col-sm-12">
      <div class="blog-information">
        <h1 class="font-weight-bold mb-3">{{blog.title}}</h1>
        <p>{{blog.content|truncatewords:30}}</p>
        <a href="{% url 'blogs_detail' blog.pk %}" class="font-weight-bold mb-3 d-inline-
block">
          Read More
        </a>
        <div class="update-edit">
          {% if request.user.is_authenticated and request.user == blog.author  %}
          <a class="btn btn-sm btn-info" href="{% url 'blog_update' blog.pk %}">Update</a>
          <a class="btn btn-sm btn-danger" href="{% url 'blog_delete' blog.pk
%}">Delete</a>
          {% endif %}
        </div>
      </div>
    </div>
  </div>
  {% endfor %}
  <div class="pagination">
    <span class="step-links">
      {% if page_obj.has_previous %}
      <div class="step-divider">
        <a href="?page=1">« first</a>
        <a href="?page={{ page_obj.previous_page_number }}">previous</a>
      </div>
      {% endif %}
      <span class="current">
        Page {{ page_obj.number }} of {{ page_obj.paginator.num_pages }}.
      </span>
      {% if page_obj.has_next %}
      <div class="step-divider">
        <a href="?page={{ page_obj.next_page_number }}">next</a>
        <a href="?page={{ page_obj.paginator.num_pages }}">last »</a>
```

```
        </div>
      {% endif %}
    </span>
  </div>
  {% else %}
  <h2 class="text-muted text-center">It's pretty lonely to have no blogs on a blogging
site</h2>
    <p class="mt-3 h3 text-muted text-center">Add a blog? <a href="{% url 'blog_create'
%}">Click here</a></p>
    {% endif %}
</div>
{% endblock content %}
```

Code 58 financeblog\blog\templates\blog\blog_list.html

Our new **blog_list.html** template is quite similar to the **list.html** template we previously used, but we've added more content to this one. We are now displaying the image of the author as well as a link to their profile. Note that the blog has an author field which is a User. The User has a one to one relationship with the Profile model. Since these are all related, we can retrieve data of related models pretty easily by treating them as python objects like "**{{blog.user.profile.image.url}}**".

We have also added a link to the update and delete a view of the blogs. These will only be shown if the current user viewing the site is the author of the blog because of the conditional we added.

Next, we have added the code for the pagination, which is available under **page_obj** variable. Using it, we are displaying the current pagination page we are on by the **page_obj.number.** We are then adding two conditionals to check if there is a "next" or "previous" pagination page.

Lastly, we have added a conditional on adding a message if there are no blogs int the database. The queryset sent to the templates in views created from **ListView** generic view is called **object_list.** Open http://localhost:8000/

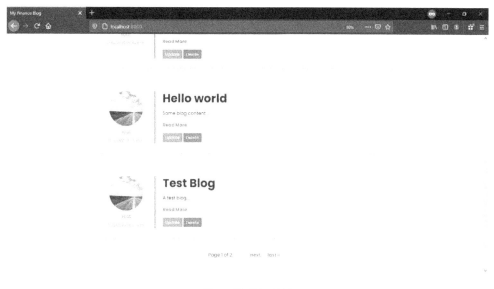

Figure 62 Object List

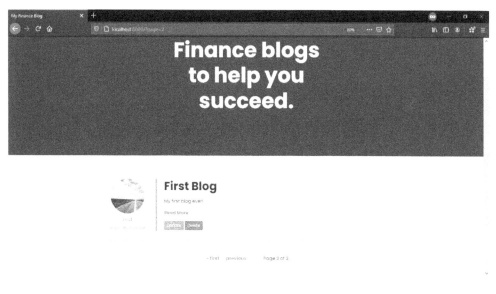

Figure 63 Single Blog

It looks perfect now. Clicking on the image or the username will lead you to the profile page. The pagination is working correctly. In this view, I chose to only display up to 3 blogs per page, and you can see that it works as expected. The update and delete buttons are clickable because the current logged-in user created these blogs.

If you log out and visit the page as guest or another user, you will see that the buttons are no longer visible.

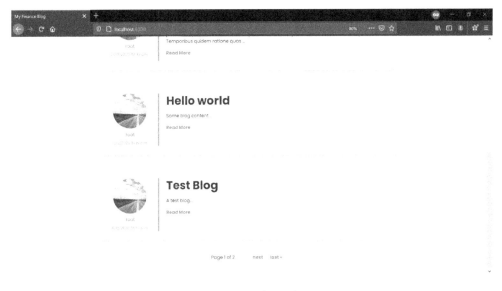

Figure 64 Logged Out View

BLOG DETAIL VIEW

GENERIC DETAIL VIEW

In the 2nd chapter, we created the detail view for blogs with the name **detail_blog**. Let's use the generic **DetailView** to create it instead. Remove the **detail_blog** view from the **views.py** file of the **blog** application and create a new view.

```
class BlogDetailView(generic.DetailView):
    model = Blog
```

The **model** attribute is required by views inheriting from the generic **DetailView**. This is all the code we need - isn't it awesome? Let's add this view to a URL pattern inside the **urls.py** file of the **blog** application. Find the following URL pattern which uses our old **detail_blog**:

```
path("blog/<int:pk>", views.detail_blog, name="blogs_detail")
```

Now change it so it uses our **BlogDetailView**:

```
path("blog/<int:pk>", views.BlogDetailView.as_view(), name="blogs_detail"),
```

Code 59 financeblog\profiles\views.py

The BlogDetailView expects a pk parameter, passed in the request from the URL, so we've added that here.

TEMPLATE FOR GENERIC DETAIL VIEW

According to the naming convention for generic views, BlogDetailView will look for it's template under "**blog/blog_detail.html**". Remove the old **detail.html** inside **templates>blog** directory of the **blog** application and create a new file called **blog_detail.html**. Add the following code to it:

```
{% extends "blog/base.html" %}
{% block content %}
<div class="container blog bg-light p-5 mt-5 rounded ">
    <div class="row">
        <div class="col-3 text-center">
            <a class="mugshot-container mb-1" href="{% url 'profile' blog.author.pk %}">
                <div class="mugshot-img mb-2" style="background-
image:url({{blog.author.profile.image.url}})"></div>
                    <span>{{blog.author.username}}</span>
            </a>
                <small class="text-muted">{{blog.date_published|date:"d/m/Y h:i a"}}</small>
        </div>
        <div class="col-9 question-information pb-1">
            <h1 class="blog-card-title mb-3 font-weight-bold">{{blog.title}}</h1>
            {% if request.user == blog.author %}
                <a href="{% url 'blog_update' blog.pk %}" class="btn btn-sm btn-
primary"> Update</a>
                    <a href="{% url 'blog_delete' blog.pk %}" class="btn btn-sm btn-
danger"> Delete</a>
            {% endif %}
        </div>
    </div>
    <div class="row">
        <div class="col-12 mt-5">
            <p class="line-height text-justify"> {{blog.content}}</p>
        </div>
    </div>
</div>
{% endblock content %}
```

Code 60 financeblog\blog\templates\blog\blog_detail.html

This template is not much different from the **detail.html** we used previously for the blog detail page. We are now displaying the author image and adding a link to their profile. We have also added the **update** and **delete** button, but these will only be shown if the current user viewing the template is the author of the blog. This is how it'll look now:

Figure 65 Detailed blog view

BLOG CONTENT LENGTH

There is currently a problem with our blog model. There is no minimum word limit for our blog. A user can create a blog that only says "hello" in the body.

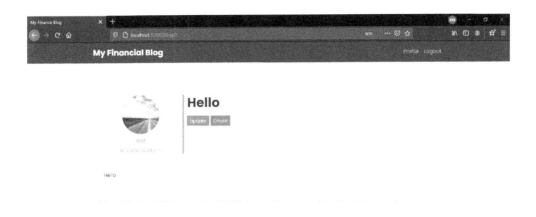

Figure 66 Any length allowable

This is bad as no blogs are only one word long. We need to verify that the content of the blog is at least 300 characters long.

We can do it at the form level or the model level. If we do it at the form level, the admin will still post blogs less than 300 characters long from the admin site or the shell.

That is why we will add this validation to our model. Before we make this change, delete all the existing blogs so we can start fresh. Best do it from the admin site.

Figure 67 Adding validation

After deleting all the blogs, opening the homepage should display a slightly depressive but encouraging message.

Figure 68 No blog in a site message

If you remember, we added a condition in the **blog_list.html** to display this message if no blogs are found where **object_list** is a list full of Blog Objects.

```
{% if object_list.count > 0 %}
        ...
{% else %}
        <h2 class="text-muted text-
center">It's pretty lonely to have no blogs on a blogging site</h2>
        ...
{% endif %}
```

Code 61 financeblog\blog\templates\blog\blog_list.html

BLOG CONTENT LENGTH VALIDATOR

Now we are ready to make the changes. Close the development server and open the **models.py** file of the **blog** application. Import the following validation function:

```
from django.core.validators import MinLengthValidator
```

Now add the following code before defining the Blog model class:

```
content_validator = MinLengthValidator(limit_value=300, message="Content should be at leas
t 300 characters long!")
```

Code 62 financeblog\blog\models.py

MinLengthValidator takes two parameters, limit_value and message. We are creating a validator and setting the minimum character limit to 300. We are also adding a message to display in case the validation fails. We are storing this validator inside the **content_validator** variable. Now add the **content_validator** to the **content** attribute of the model:

```
content = models.TextField(validators=[content_validator])
```

Our content field will now use this validator. After making the above changes, your models.py file should look like this:

```
from django.db import models
from django.utils import timezone
from django.contrib.auth.models import User
from django.urls import reverse
from django.core.validators import MinLengthValidator

content_validator = MinLengthValidator(limit_value=300, message="Content should be at leas
t 300 characters long!")

class Blog(models.Model):
    title = models.CharField(max_length=250)
    content = models.TextField(validators=[content_validator])
    date_published = models.DateTimeField(default=timezone.now)
    author = models.ForeignKey(User, on_delete=models.CASCADE)
    def __str__(self):
        return self.title
    def get_absolute_url(self):
        return reverse("blogs_detail", kwargs={'pk': self.pk})
```

Code 63 financeblog\blog\models.py

Now that we have altered a field on the model, we need to run the migrations. Run the **makemigrations** command:

Terminal

```
(MyProject) E:\MyProject\financeblog>python manage.py makemigrations
Migrations for 'blog':
  blog\migrations\0002_auto_20201218_1938.py
    - Alter field content on blog
```

It created migrations. Now we need to run the **migrate** command to push these model changes to our blog schema in the database:

```
(MyProject) E:\MyProject\financeblog>python manage.py migrate
Operations to perform:
  Apply all migrations: admin, auth, blog, contenttypes, profiles, sessions
Running migrations:
  Applying blog.0002_auto_20201218_1938... OK
```

Now run the development server and visit http://localhost:8000/blog/create. Try creating a blog and no providing enough words for the title, you'll see an error message like the one on the following Figure. Form Validation: Check!

Figure 69 Validation rule on blog creation

BLOG CREATION LINK

One final touch before moving on to the next Chapter. Currently, there is no link on our website that leads to the blog creation page. Open the **base.html** template inside the **templates>blog** directory of the blog application and replace the html **header** tag with the code below:

```html
<header>
  <nav class="navbar navbar-expand-lg navbar-dark bg-dark">
    <div class="container">
      <a class="navbar-brand mb-0 h1" href="{% url 'blog_list' %}">My Financial Blog</a>
      <button class="navbar-toggler" type="button" data-toggle="collapse" data-
target="#navbarSupportedContent"
        aria-controls="navbarSupportedContent" aria-expanded="false" aria-label="Toggle
navigation">
        <span class="navbar-toggler-icon"></span>
      </button>
      <div class="collapse navbar-collapse" id="navbarSupportedContent">
        <ul class="navbar-nav">
          <li class="nav-item ml-2">
            <a href="{% url 'blog_create' %}" class="nav-link btn btn-dark">Write a
Blog</a>
          </li>
        </ul>
        <ul class="navbar-nav ml-auto">
          {% if request.user.is_authenticated %}
          <li class="nav-item">
            <a href="{% url 'profile' request.user.pk %}" class="nav-link">Profile</a>
          </li>
          <li class="nav-item">
            <a href="{% url 'logout' %}" class="nav-link">Logout</a>
          </li>
          {% else %}
          <li class="nav-item">
            <a href="{% url 'login' %}" class="nav-link">Login</a>
          </li>
          <li class="nav-item">
            <a href="{% url 'register' %}" class="nav-link">Register</a>
          </li>
          {% endif %}
        </ul>
      </div>
    </div>
  </nav>
</header>
```

Code 64 financeblog\blog\templates\blog\base.html

We've only added one new link, but just for simplicity's sake and so you know where to put the link, we are showing the full header tag. Your navbar should now have a minimalistic looking "Write a Blog" button.

Testing Blog Content Limit

Lorem ipsum dolor, sit amet consectetur adipisicing elit. Harum omnis nihil debitis esse voluptatibus ut molestias incidunt alias veritatis nisi. Incidunt consequatur quasi obcaecati quae

Figure 70 Availability of the button "Write a blog."

ADVICE

Our website is complete. Users can register, upload images and descriptions about themselves. Users can post blogs and update/delete their own blogs. They cannot update/delete blogs of other users.

It's time we add the **advice** section. We will now add a feature so users can post a **question,** and others can provide their advice. We will also look at how to create a REST API using the Django Rest Framework.

ADVICE APPLICATION

You know the drill, close the development server and create a new application by the name of **advice**. Before you read any further, if you are sitting in front of your Machine, try and do it yourself. Use the "help" command in "python manage.py" if necessary.

Terminal

```
(MyProject) E:\MyProject\financeblog>python manage.py startapp advice
```

Make sure to add it to the **INSTALLED_APPS** setting in the **settings.py** file inside the **financeblog** directory:

```
INSTALLED_APPS = [
    'django.contrib.admin',
    'django.contrib.auth',
    'django.contrib.contenttypes',
    'django.contrib.sessions',
    'django.contrib.messages',
    'django.contrib.staticfiles',
    'blog',
    'profiles',
    'crispy_forms',
    'advice'
]
```

QUESTION AND ANSWER SCHEMA

Our advice applications will have two models, **Question** and **Advice**. There will be a one-to-many relation between the two, i.e. a question can have much advice, but advice can only belong to a single question.

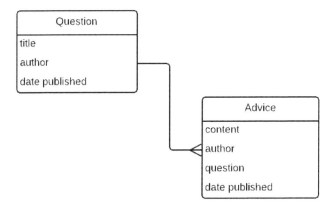

Figure 71 One to Many relationships between question and advice

Our **Question** and **Advice** models will also share a one-to-many relation with the **User** model. Open the **models.py** file of the **advice** application and add the following code:

```
from django.db import models
from django.contrib.auth.models import User
from django.utils import timezone
from django.urls import reverse

class Question(models.Model):
    title = models.CharField(max_length=500)
    author = models.ForeignKey(User, on_delete=models.CASCADE)
    date_published = models.DateTimeField(default=timezone.now)

    def __str__(self):
        return self.title

class Advice(models.Model):
    content = models.TextField()
    author = models.ForeignKey(User, on_delete=models.CASCADE)
    question = models.ForeignKey(Question, on_delete=models.CASCADE)
    date_published = models.DateTimeField(default=timezone.now)

    def __str__(self):
        return f"Advice by {self.author.username}"
```

Code 65 financeblog\profiles\models.py

Let's go over the the field **Question** model first.

- **title**: It is a CharField with a max_length of 500.
- **author**: It is a ForeignKey which means that question shares a one-to-many relation with the User model. Through **on_delete=models.CASCADE,** we are ensuring that in case the user is deleted, the question gets deleted too.
- **date_published**: It is a DateTimeField, and we are setting it defaults to **timezone.now.**Upon creation of an instance of **Question**, the attribute will automatically be set to the current time.
- Lastly, we are returning the title of the question through the **__str__** method.

Fields of the **Advice** model:

- **content**: It is of type TextField. This is the body of the answer.
- **author**: It is the same as the author field on the **Question** model.
- **question:** We are defining a ForeignKey(one-to-many) relation between the **Question** and the **Answer**. The **on_delete=models.CASCADE** means that in

case a question is deleted, we also want to delete the answer associated with that question.

- **date_published:** It is a DateTimeField, the same as on our **Question** model.
- Lastly, we are returning the name of the user through the **__str__** method.

Our Schema is written down. It it isn't reflected in the Database though. Remember, in order for these fields to go from Python Code to SQL Fields inside a PostgreSQL Server, we need to generate and run the migrations.

Terminal

```
(MyProject) E:\MyProject\financeblog>python manage.py makemigrations
Migrations for 'advice':
  advice\migrations\0001_initial.py
    - Create model Question
    - Create model Advice
```

Terminal

```
(MyProject) E:\MyProject\financeblog>python manage.py migrate
Operations to perform:
  Apply all migrations: admin, advice, auth, blog, contenttypes, profiles, sessions
Running migrations:
  Applying advice.0001_initial... OK
```

REGISTERING MODELS IN THE ADMIN SITE

Open the **admin.py** file inside the **advice** application and register the **Question** and **Advice** model we just created. If your site is going to have a lot of Models and you want them All to be in the Admin Panel, you might as well write a simple Python script, that will import all Classes from the models.py files and pass them into admin.site.register as Array.

```
from django.contrib import admin
from .models import Question, Advice
admin.site.register(Question)
admin.site.register(Advice)
```

Code 66 financeblog\profiles\admin.py

You can also pass a list of Models to the **admin.site.register()**. Open the admin site at http://localhost:8000/admin, and you should now see the **Question** and **Advice**.

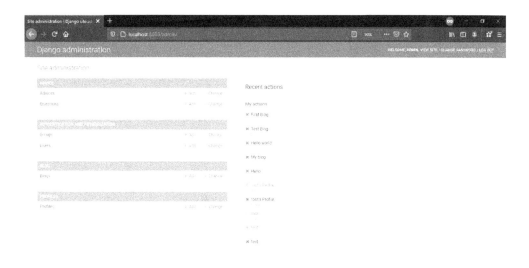

Figure 72 Question and advice view in Admin side

You can try adding or deleting the **Question** and **Advice** instances. We will now begin creating class-based generic views for the **Question** model.

VIEWS

QUESTION CREATE VIEW

Let's start by creating the create view of our **Question** model. Add the following code to the **views.py** file of the **advice** application:

```python
from django.views import generic
from django.contrib.auth.mixins import LoginRequiredMixin
from django.contrib.messages.views import SuccessMessageMixin
from .models import Question

class QuestionCreateView(LoginRequiredMixin, SuccessMessageMixin, generic.CreateView):
    model = Question
    fields = ['title']
    success_message = "Question Created Successfully!"

    def form_valid(self, form):
        form.instance.author = self.request.user
        return super().form_valid(form)
```

Code 67 financeblog\profiles\views.py

We have created a view called **QuestionCreateView** that extends from **CreateView** generic view. It is the same as our **BlogCreateView**. We are passing the field **title** in the **fields** attribute. We are also using **LoginRequiredMixin** and **SuccessMessageMixin**. There is nothing new here. Let's create the URL pattern for our **QuestionCreateView**.

First create the **urls.py** file inside the **advice** application and add the following code to it:

```
from django.urls import path
from . import views
urlpatterns = [
    path('create/', views.QuestionCreateView.as_view(), name="question_create"),
]
```

Code 68 financeblog\financeblog\urls.py

Now let's add the URL patterns of our **advice** application inside the **urls.py** file of the project. Add the following pattern inside the URL patterns list in the **urls.py** file of **financeblog** directory:

```
path('questions/', include('advice.urls'))
```

It means our **QuestionCreateView** view will be available under the path "questions/create". We have linked the urls.py file of our advice application with the URL patterns of the project. As per the naming convention of the generic class-based views, **QuestionCreateView** will look for its template under "**advice/question_form.html**".

Let's start by creating the directories for the templates. Inside the **advice** application, create a directory called **templates**, and inside the templates directory create a directory called **advice**. Inside the **advice** directory create a file called **question_form.html**. After making the changes, the templates directory of the **advice** application should have the following directory structure:

Add the following code to **question_form.html**:

```
{% extends "blog/base.html" %}
{% load crispy_forms_tags %}
{% block content %}
<div class="landing bg-dark">
  <div class="container">
    <div class="row align-items-center justify-content-center">
      <div class="col-sm-12 col-lg-6 text-center">
        <h1 class="text-white font-weight-bold display-3 mb-3">Have a Question?</h1>
      </div>
    </div>
  </div>
</div>
<div class="container bg-light mt-n5 p-5 rounded ">
  <div class="row">
    <div class="col-12">
      <form method="POST">
        {% csrf_token %}
        {{form|crispy}}
        <div class="form-group">
          <button class="btn btn-outline-dark">Submit</button>
        </div>
      </form>
    </div>
  </div>
</div>
{% endblock content %}
```

Code 69 financeblog\advice\templates\advice\question_form.html

This code is the same as our **blog_form.html** template. We've just copied and pasted
that same code. The only thing we've changed is the heading which now says, "Have
a question?". Let's test it by visiting http://localhost:8000/questions/create.

Figure 73 Question submission form

Figure 74 Error from the Question Model

This error was expected as we've not created the **get_absolute_url** method on the Question model yet. Our question was saved successfully, and you can verify it through the admin site.

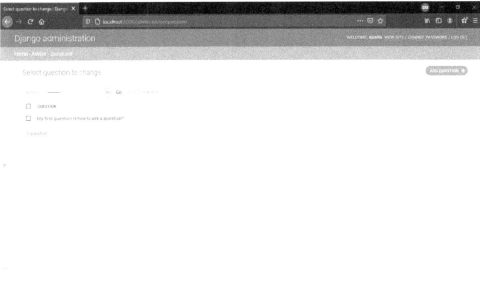

Figure 75 Question generated in the admin side

Since we don't have a detailed view of the Question model yet, we will postpone creating the get_absolute_url when we create the detail view.

QUESTION UPDATE VIEW

We will not be creating an updated view of the questions. Suppose a user posted a question and others offer their advice. After some users have posted their advice, the question's original poster updates the question so now. It is asking something entirely different. The answers provided on the question page will not make any sense. Therefore, we will not be creating an update page for the question.

The admin will still be able to make changes through the admin site. Besides, you have bravely made it until this Chapter. So you know very well how to create your own (generic) Update View.

QUESTION DELETE VIEW

Inside **views.py** of the **advice** application, add the following import:

```
from django.contrib import messages
```

Now add the following code:

```
class QuestionDeleteView(LoginRequiredMixin, UserPassesTestMixin, generic.DeleteView):
    model = Question
    success_message  = "Question Deleted Successfully!"
    success_url = "/questions"

    def test_func(self):
        question = self.get_object()
        if self.request.user == question.author:
            return True
        else:
            return False

    def delete(self, request, *args, **kwargs):
        messages.success(self.request, self.success_message)
        return super(QuestionDeleteView, self).delete(request, *args, **kwargs)
```

Code 70 financeblog\advice\views.py

This view is the same as our **BlogDeleteView**. The only difference is that we are now passing the **Question** model. Using the **UserPassesTestMixin**, we are ensuring that only the author of the question can delete it. Note that we are redirecting to a path "/questions" which is where we will list our questions. It currently doesn't exist to get a 404 page after you delete a question and are redirected.

Let's create a URL pattern for our QuestionDeleteView. Open the **urls.py** file of the **advice** application and add the following URL pattern to the urlpatterns list:

```
path('<int:pk>/delete', views.QuestionDeleteView.as_view(), name="question_delete"),
```

Our **QuestionDeleteView** will look for a template by the name **question_confirm_delete.html**. Let's add it. Inside the **templates>advice** directory of the **advice** application, add a file called **question_confirm_delete.html** and add the following markup to it:

```
{% extends "blog/base.html" %}
{% load crispy_forms_tags %}
{% block content %}
<div class="container bg-light p-5 mt-5 rounded ">
  <div class="row">
    <div class="col-12">
      <h2>Are you sure you want to delete the question
"<strong>{{object.title}}</strong>"?</h2>
      <form method="POST">
        {% csrf_token %}
        <div class="form-group">
          <button class="btn btn-danger">Yes please.</button>
          <a class="btn btn-info" href="#">No, take me back</a>
        </div>
      </form>
    </div>
  </div>
</div>
{% endblock content %}
```

Code 71 financeblog\advice\templates\advice\question_confirm_delete.html

Again, we've just copy-pasted the **blog_confirm_delete.html** template. Note that the "No, take me back" link doesn't take you anywhere as we have yet to create the detail page of the question.

Figure 76 Delete view of the questions

QUESTION DETAIL VIEW

If you remember, the generic detail View is among the most complex and hard to remember views. Add the following code to the **views.py** file of the **advice** application.

```
class QuestionDetailView(generic.DetailView):
    model = Question
```

Open **urls.py** file of the **advice** application. Add the following URL pattern to the urlpatterns list:

```
path('<int:pk>/', views.QuestionDetailView.as_view(), name="question_detail"),
```

By naming convention, **QuestionDetailView** will look for its template under "**advice/question_detail.html**". Inside the **templates>advice** directory of the **advice** application, create a file called **question_detail.html**. Insert the following code.

245

```
{% extends "blog/base.html" %}
{% block content %}
<div class="container blog bg-light p-5 mt-5 rounded">
  <div class="row">
    <div class="col-3 text-center">
      <a class="mugshot-container mb-1" href="{% url 'profile' question.author.pk %}">
        <div class="mugshot-img mb-2" style="background-
image:url({{question.author.profile.image.url}})"></div>
        <span>{{question.author.username}}</span>
      </a>
      <small class="text-muted">{{question.date_published|date:"d/m/Y h:i a"}}</small>
    </div>
    <div class="col-9 question-information pb-1">
      <div class="question">
        <div class="question-mark">
          <span>Q:</span>
        </div>
        <div class="question-content">
          <h3 class="mb-0">{{question.title}}</h3>

        </div>
      </div>
      {% if request.user == question.author %}
      <div class="pl-2">
        <a href="{% url 'question_delete' question.pk %}" class="btn btn-sm btn-danger">
Delete</a>
      </div>
      {% endif %}
    </div>
  </div>
</div>
{% endblock content %}
```

Code 72 financeblog\advice\templates\advice\question_detail.html

This template is very similar to the **blog_detail.html**. We have changed some styling here and there and are displaying the question title, date_publsihed, and the author's information. We've also added the **delete** button, which links to the delete page of this question. Note that it will only be shown if the current logged in user is the author of the question. Open http://localhost:8000/questions/1.

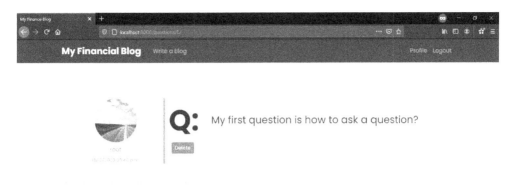

Let's add a link for this view inside our **question_confirm_delete.html**. Open **question_confirm_delete.html** and find where it says "No, take me back".

```
<a class="btn btn-info" href="#">No, take me back</a>
```

Change the href, so it now points to our detail page:

```
<a class="btn btn-
info" href="{% url 'question_detail' question.pk %}">No, take me back</a>
```

Code 73 financeblog\advice\templates\advice\question_confirm_delete.html

Let's also create the **get_absolute_url** method now that we have a detail page for the question model. Open the **models.py** file of the **advice** application and the following method to the **Question** class:

```
def get_absolute_url(self):
        return reverse("question_detail", kwargs={'pk': self.pk})
```

Code 74 financeblog\advice\models.py

We are creating the URL using the **reverse** function. Creating a new question should redirect us to its detail page now.

QUESTION LIST VIEW

Open **views.py** file of the **advice** application and add the following code:

```
class QuestionListView(generic.ListView):
    model = Question
    paginate_by = 3
    ordering = ['-date_published']
```

Code 75 financeblog\advice\views.py

We have created the **QuestionListView** by extending from the generic ListView. Just like we did in **BlogListView**, we are also adding the pagination and ordering attributes to the **QuestionListView**. Open the **urls.py** file of the **advice** application and add the following URL pattern to the URL patterns list.

```
path('',views.QuestionListView.as_view(),name="question_list"),
```

Our **QuestionListView** view will be available under the "questions/" path. It will look for a template by the name of "**question_list.html**". Add a file called **question_list.html** to the **templates>advice** directory inside the **advice** application and insert the following code.

```
{% extends "blog/base.html" %}
{% block content %}
<div class="landing bg-dark">
  <div class="container">
    <div class="row align-items-center justify-content-center">
      <div class="col-sm-12 col-lg-6 text-center">
        <h1 class="text-white font-weight-bold display-3 mb-3">Help others succeed in
finance.</h1>
      </div>
    </div>
  </div>
</div>
<div class="container p-5 rounded ">
  {% if object_list.count > 0 %}
  {% for question in object_list %}
  <div class="row blog mb-5">
    <div class="col-lg-2 col-sm-12 text-center">
      <a class="mugshot-container mb-1" href="{% url 'profile' question.author.pk %}">
        <div class="mugshot-img mb-2" style="background-
image:url({{question.author.profile.image.url}})"></div>
        <span>{{question.author.username}}</span>
      </a>
      <small class="text-muted">{{question.date_published|date:"d/m/Y h:i a"}}</small>
    </div>
    <div class="col-lg-10 col-sm-12">
      <div class="blog-information">
        <h3 class="font-weight-bold mb-3">{{question.title}}</h3>
        <a href="{% url 'question_detail' question.pk %}" class="font-weight-bold mb-3 d-
inline-block">
        Read Thread
        </a>
        <div class="update-edit">
          {% if request.user.is_authenticated and request.user == question.author  %}
          <a class="btn btn-sm btn-danger" href="{% url 'question_delete' question.pk
%}">Delete</a>
          {% endif %}
        </div>
      </div>
    </div>
  </div>
  {% endfor %}
  <div class="pagination">
    <span class="step-links">
      {% if page_obj.has_previous %}
      <div class="step-divider">
        <a href="?page=1">« first</a>
        <a href="?page={{ page_obj.previous_page_number }}">previous</a>
      </div>
      {% endif %}
      <span class="current">
        Page {{ page_obj.number }} of {{ page_obj.paginator.num_pages }}.
      </span>
      {% if page_obj.has_next %}
      <div class="step-divider">
        <a href="?page={{ page_obj.next_page_number }}">next</a>
        <a href="?page={{ page_obj.paginator.num_pages }}">last »</a>
      </div>
      {% endif %}
    </span>
  </div>
  {% else %}
  <h2 class="text-muted text-center">No queries posted yet...</h2>
```

```
    <p class="mt-3 h3 text-muted text-center">Ask a question? <a href="{% url
'question_create' %}">Click here</a></p>
    {% endif %}
</div>
{% endblock content %}
```

Code 76 financeblog\blog\templates\blog\blog_list.html

Again, this code layout is the same as our **blog_list.html** template. We've only changed the variables to match the question. We've changed a few things, i.e. changed the main heading and changed the question title's size. Everything else, as you can see, is pretty much boilerplate. Meaning, you can use it for other List Views - simply adjust the wording. Open http://localhost:8000/questions.

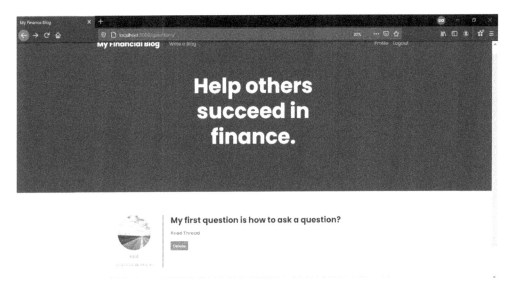

Figure 78 Word adjustment

Let's update the navigation bar while we are at it. Open the **base.html** file inside the **templates > blog** directory of the **blog** application and find the HTML header code. Find the last </li> and {% endif %} tag. Insert another link after the endif-condition.

```
<header>
...
{% endif %}
<li class="nav-item">
    <a href="{% url 'question_list' %}" class="nav-link">Browse Questions</a>
</li>
...
</header>
```

Code 77 financeblog\blog\templates\blog\base.html

We have added two new links to create a question and one link that takes you to the **QuestionListView** page.

Figure 79 New button added for asking a question

TESTING QUESTION VIEWS

Let's create the views of the Question models. Open
http://localhost:8000/questions/create

Figure 80 View for the question model

After creating the question, you should be redirected to its detail page.

Figure 81 Question created successfully

Django 3 for Beginners

Let's delete this question.

Are you sure you want to delete the question "**How to do taxes?**"?

Yes please   No, take me back

Figure 82 Question delete view

If you press the "No, Take me back" button, you'll be taken back to the detail page. If you delete the question, you will be redirected to the question list page.

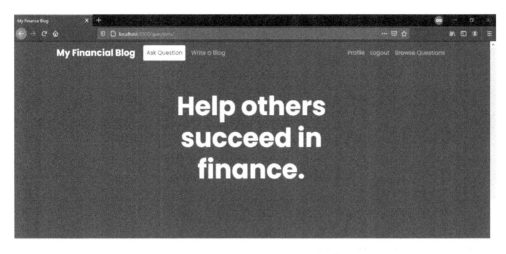

Question Deleted Successfully! ✕

| My first question is how to ask a question?

Figure 83 Question deleted successfully

REST API - DRF

DECOUPLING BACKEND & FRONTEND

INTRODUCTION

Say, for our web app, you build a mobile application. You want to display all the questions on our website, but how will you get data from the web application? The mobile application and web application are two different applications and are not connected in any way. You can scrap the site. You can directly connect with the database but will need to build an additional backend for processing the data. These or several different methods which are all hacky ways to get the data.

Enter REST APIs. We can create a REST API in our web application that will return the questions on our web application in a JSON format. Let's say we created the API on the path "/questions/api/all".

Now, suppose you perform an HTTP GET request against this endpoint. In that case, it doesn't matter if you are on a browser, or performing the request through the curl terminal command, or performing the HTTP request through AJAX. You will always get the data back in JSON format. This way, we can expose our application's data straightforwardly, so it is available to other platforms.

HTTP Method

REST APIs allow us to build URL endpoints that will return or accept data in a universal format, usually JSON. We will not go into the jargon as REST is a topic of its own, but we will briefly explain it to give you an idea.

OUR USE CASE

We will create two views for the **Advice** model, allowing users to create advice for a question and list all of the advice for a given question. Both create and list views of advice will be displayed on the detail page of the Question model. However, we don't want to build these the traditional way.

Suppose you go to any modern website which has a comment system. In that case, you will notice that your comment gets added without the page reloading.

This creates a pleasant user experience as the page doesn't reload, and the user can keep doing what they were doing. You must also have noticed that the comment section is loaded on some websites when you scroll down to it, meaning it fetches data in real-time from the server. This instant feedback on the action is very welcomed by users and is pretty much status quo today.

AJAX & DJANGO VIEWS

This is all done by performing HTTP requests through AJAX calls on the page or, more specifically, the API. These HTTP requests are made to URL endpoints accepting and returning data in JSON instead of HTML documents. We need to build some kind of API on our web application that will allow the user to retrieve the advice of a question in JSON format and send JSON data to an Endpoint. This Endpoint will create the specified advice for a particular question.

DJANGO REST FRAMEWORK (DRF)

WHY DRF?

To create REST APIs, we will utilize the Django REST Framework (DRF). DRF allows us to implement REST in a Django project very quickly. It comes with a set of valuable features we otherwise would have to implement ourselves. It is used inside a Django Project, i.e., it doesn't work standalone. It offers various features such as views, generic views, authentication, serialization, browsable API, and a lot more.

It also comes with very in-depth documentation that covers every topic in detail. We will only be scratching the DRF's surface in our project. It is a complete framework dedicated to only creating REST APIs in Django.

INSTALLING DJANGO REST FRAMEWORK

Close the development server and install the Django rest framework.

```
(MyProject) E:\MyProject\financeblog>pip install djangorestframework
```

Next, add it to the **INSTALLED_APP** setting in the **settings.py** file of the project.

```
INSTALLED_APPS = [
    'django.contrib.admin',
    'django.contrib.auth',
    'django.contrib.contenttypes',
    'django.contrib.sessions',
    'django.contrib.messages',
    'django.contrib.staticfiles',
    'blog',
    'profiles',
    'crispy_forms',
    'advice',
    'rest_framework'
]
```

CREATING ADVICE LIST VIEW

Open **views.py** of the **advice** application and add the following imports.

```
from .models import Advice
from rest_framework.views import APIView
from rest_framework.response import Response
from rest_framework.reverse import reverse
from django.utils import formats
```

Code 78 financeblog\advice\views.py

Now we'll create a View, similar to the Views we created earlier.

```
class AdviceListView(APIView):
    def get(self, request, pk=None):
        queryset = Advice.objects.all().filter(question_id=pk).order_by("-date_published")
        data_to_return = []

        for advice in queryset:
            username = advice.author.username
            user_url = request.build_absolute_uri(reverse('profile', args=[advice.author.p
k]))
            user_image = request.build_absolute_uri(advice.author.profile.image.url)
            content = advice.content
            date_published = formats.date_format(advice.date_published, "SHORT_DATETIME_FO
RMAT")
            instance = {
                'username' : username,
                'user_url': user_url,
                'user_image': user_image,
                'content': content,
                'date_published': date_published
            }
            data_to_return.append(instance)
        return Response(data_to_return)
```

Code 79 financeblog\advice\views.py

We are creating the **AdviceListView** view that extends from django-rest-framework's **APIView**. This view will respond to GET requests only. That is why we only have a **get** method. If we want to perform actions on other HTTP calls such as POST or DELETE to this view, we will have to create a class method by the name of the HTTP request type, which will handle the code of that scenario.

We are passing three parameters to the **get** method, i.e., **self, request,** and **pk**. Our view will get the **pk** parameter through the URL. Next, we have this line of code.

```
queryset = Advice.objects.all().filter(question_id=pk).order_by("-date_published")
```

We are retrieving all the instances of the Advice model that belong to a particular question. We are filtering that question by its id and passing the **pk** parameter we received as the matching query. Next, we are ordering the queryset result by the most recent advice published through the **date_published** field.

259

We are creating an empty list by the name **data_to_return** and looping over the queryset we just made. We are then retrieving some data, and these are:

```
username = advice.author.username
```

We are storing the username of the author of the advice.

```
user_url = request.build_absolute_uri(reverse('profile', args=[advice.author.pk]))
```

We are creating a URL for the profile of the author with the **reverse** method. We are passing '**profile**', which is the name of the user's profile URL. We are passing it the pk of the author of the advice as well so it knows which user we are talking about. Lastly, we are wrapping the reverse method inside the build_absolute_uri method, which will create the full absolute URL as reverse only creates a partial relative URL.

```
user_image = request.build_absolute_uri(advice.author.profile.image.url)
```

Here we are creating the URL link of the author's profile image. We are building it the same way we did in the previous step.

```
content = advice.content
```

We are storing the content of the advice instance.

```
date_published = formats.date_format(advice.date_published, "SHORT_DATETIME_FORMAT")
```

We are storing the **date_published** field of the advice instance but by default, it will return in a different format. We are wrapping it inside the **date_format** function and specifying that we want the '**SHORT_DATETIME_FORMAT**' format.

```
instance = {
  'username' : username,
  'user_url': user_url,
  'user_image': user_image,
  'content': content,
  'date_published': date_published
}
```

In this piece of code, we are creating an instance of the advice we want to send back through the URL. It is a python dictionary, and it holds all the variables we just created.

```
data_to_return.append(instance)
```

Lastly, we are appending the instance dictionary to the **data_to_return** list we created earlier. Remember that we were looping over the queryset, so it will create this instance for all the advice the queryset has.

```
return Response(data_to_return)
```

Finally, we are sending the data back through the Response method. Note that this Response method will automatically convert our python dictionary to a JSON object.

ADVICE LIST VIEW URL PATTERN

Let's create a URL pattern for our **AdviceListView**. Open the **urls.py** file of the **advice** application and add the following URL pattern to the URL patterns list.

```
path('api/<int:pk>', views.AdviceListView.as_view()),
```

Code 80 financeblog\advice\urls.py

Remember, our view was using a pk for querying a specific question. It will get that parameter from our URL.

ADVICE LIST VIEW TESTING

Visit the **Question** section in the admin site and add a new question.

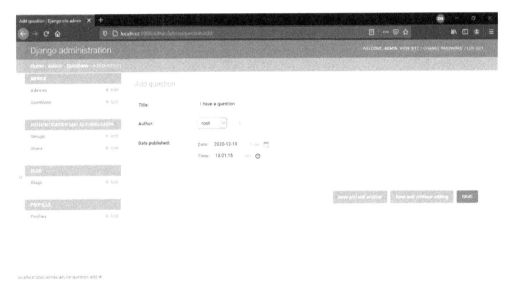

Figure 84 Question section in the admin site

Let's also add a few advice to this question through the admin site.

Django 3 for Beginners

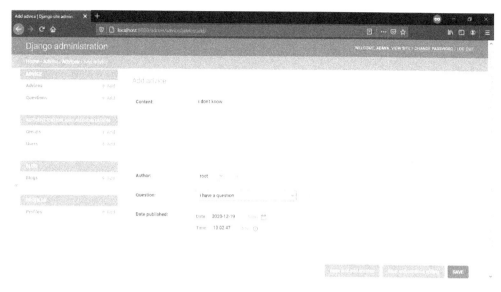

Figure 85 Adding new advice

Note the id of the question you just created and visit
http://localhost:8000/questions/api/3. Note that "3" here refers to the pk of the
question we just created.

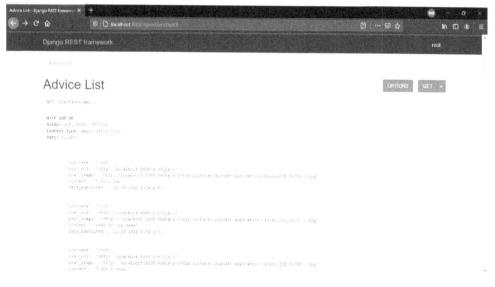

Figure 86 Django template provided by rest-framework

This template is provided by the django-rest-framework and is very good for development purposes because we can interact with the API graphically. You will want to disable this in production to only show raw JSON data.

You can see that our **AdviceListView** view is returning the data correctly. It is in JSON format. We are sending the **username, user_image** and **user_url** because we want to display the information of the advice author as well.

Note that this is a public API, meaning anyone can access this data. We don't want to protect this route as we want unauthenticated users to also be able to read comments on our web application.

ADVICE CREATE SERIALIZER

WHAT IS SERIALIZER?

Serializers convert data from JSON to python objects(called serializing) and from python objects to JSON(called de-serializing).

Figure 87 Serialization De-Serialization mechanism

They work very similarly to Django forms as we create our serializers by inheriting from either **Serializer** or **ModelSerializer** classes. We then define attributes on our serializer class and specify what sort of data that attribute should expect, i.e., whether it will be an email or a CharField etc.

The only difference between the **Serializer** and **ModelSerializer** class is that **ModelSerializer** class allows us to build a serializer based on a model that we pass it, kind of like we did in forms extending from ModelForm.

CREATE SERIALIZER

Create a file called **serializers.py** inside the advice application and add the following code to it:

```python
from rest_framework import serializers
from .models import Advice

class AdviceCreateSerializer(serializers.ModelSerializer):
    class Meta:
        model = Advice
        fields = ['content']
```

Code 81 financeblog\advice\serializers.py

This serializer will expect one field only, **content**. The advice model also has the **author, question,** and **date_published** fields, but we will handle those in the view.

CREATING ADVICE CREATE VIEW

Open the **views.py** file of the advice application and add the following imports.

```
from rest_framework import status
from .serializers import AdviceCreateSerializer
```

Code 82 financeblog\advice\views.py

Next, add the following code for the view:

```
class AdviceCreateView(APIView):
    def post(self, request, pk=None):
        if request.user.is_authenticated:
            serializer = AdviceCreateSerializer(data=request.data)
            if serializer.is_valid():
                user = request.user
                try:
                    question = Question.objects.get(pk=pk)
                except Question.DoesNotExist:
                    return Response({"error" : "Question does not exist!"},status=status.H
TTP_400_BAD_REQUEST)
                advice = Advice.objects.create(content=serializer.validated_data["content"
], author=user , question=question)
                advice.save()
                data_to_return = {
                    "username": advice.author.username,
                    "user_url": reverse('profile', args=[advice.author.pk], request=reques
t),
                    "user_image":request.build_absolute_uri(advice.author.profile.image.ur
l),
                    "content": advice.content,
                    "date_published":formats.date_format(advice.date_published, "SHORT_DAT
ETIME_FORMAT")
                }
                return Response(data_to_return, status=status.HTTP_201_CREATED)
            else:
                return Response(status=status.HTTP_400_BAD_REQUEST)
        else:
            return Response(status.HTTP_401_UNAUTHORIZED)
```

Code 83 financeblog\advice\views.py

We have created a view called **AdviceCreatView** that extends from the **APIView**. Notice that we are now defining a **post** method, not a **get**. That is because this view will only accept POST HTTP requests. We are passing the pk parameter to the view, and we will get this from the URL.

Inside the view body, The first thing we check is whether the user posting data is authenticated or not. If the user is not logged in, we are returning an HTTP 401 error.

We have created an instance of the **AdviceCreateSerializer** and are passing the data from the request.

```
serializer = AdviceCreateSerializer(data=request.data)
```

Next, we are calling the **is_valid** and checking if the user-submitted data is valid or not. If the data is not valid, we are returning an HTTP 404 error. If the form is valid, we execute the following code.

```
user = request.user
try:
    question = Question.objects.get(pk=pk)
except Question.DoesNotExist:
    return Response({"error" : "Question does not exist!"},
status=status.HTTP_400_BAD_REQUEST)
advice = Advice.objects.create(content=serializer.validated_data["content"], author=user ,
 question=question)
advice.save()
```

We are storing the currently logged-in user in the **user** variable. Next, we are fetching an instance of the Question model through the pk parameter and storing it in the question variable.

We have added a try-catch block here. Suppose the pk provided by the URL is invalid, and no question exists matching that pk. It will raise a **DoesNotExist** exception. We are catching the exception and returning a 400 bad request.

Then we are creating a new instance of the **Advice** model. We pass it the **content** field received from the user-submitted data after it's been validated, user and question. Lastly, we are calling the save method, which will create the instance for us. After we save the instance, we return a JSON or Dict Object.

```
data_to_return = {
"username": advice.author.username,
"user_url": reverse('profile', args=[advice.author.pk], request=request),
"user_image":request.build_absolute_uri(advice.author.profile.image.url),
"content": advice.content,
"date_published":formats.date_format(advice.date_published, "SHORT_DATETIME_FORMAT")
                }
return Response(data_to_return, status=status.HTTP_201_CREATED)
```

We are creating an object called **data_to_return** and passing it the newly created advice data and user information. This is the same information we were returning in our list view. The only difference is that now we are returning a single object, the newly created advice instance.

One last thing we should mention here is that our create view is a protected route. It will only work if the user is logged in. We usually use token-based authentication with REST APIs, but that is a separate topic of its own. Currently, we are relying on Django's default session-based authentication system to authenticate ourselves. This is suitable for us as we will only be performing AJAX calls right from our web application.

ADVICE CREATE VIEW URL PATTERN

Open the **urls.py** file of the advice application and add the following URL pattern to the URL patterns list and open http://localhost:8000/questions/api/3/create.

```
path('api/<int:pk>/create', views.AdviceCreateView.as_view()),
```

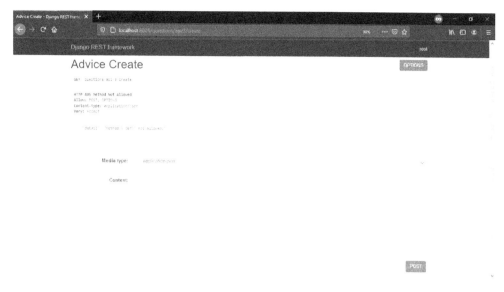

Figure 88 Without getting method view

You can see it says, "\GET not allowed". We didn't specify the **get** method on our view, and the reason it shows us this message because we performed a GET request when we opened this page. You can see the form below. Let's test our API through this form. Remember, we only need to send a single attribute, i.e., **content.**

Figure 89 Single attribute view

We've added the following JSON in the form. It has a **content** key and a message as the value. Remember, our API accepts JSON data, and this is the only field our serializer expects. You can send other fields, it wouldn't make a difference, but this field has to be sent because we would get an error otherwise.

Now hit submit, and it will create a new advice instance. The view will fetch a question by the pk we provide in the URL and set that to the advice instance's question field. It will set the currently logged-in user as the author of the advice. It will set the **content** we sent through the form as the content of the advice. Finally, it will create a new instance.

Figure 90 New instance view

After creating successfully, we will get the newly created advice back. Now visit the **AdviceListView** URL, and you should see the advice we just created displayed as JSON Object.

Figure 91 All advice list

Now that we have created the APIs, we will now access these through on-page javascript to retrieve advice and create new advice on the Question model's detail page.

EMBED ADVICES

We will now use the **AdviceListVIew** API and display all the advices of a question on the detail page of questions. Open the **question_detail.html** template inside the **templates>advice** directory of the advice application. Replace the existing code with the code below.

```
{% extends "blog/base.html" %}
{% block content %}
<div class="container blog bg-light p-5 mt-5 rounded">
  <div class="row">
    <div class="col-3 text-center">
      <a class="mugshot-container mb-1" href="{% url 'profile' question.author.pk %}">
        <div class="mugshot-img mb-2" style="background-
image:url({{question.author.profile.image.url}})"></div>
        <span>{{question.author.username}}</span>
      </a>
      <small class="text-muted">{{question.date_published|date:"d/m/Y h:i a"}}</small>
    </div>
    <div class="col-9 question-information pb-1">
      <div class="question">
        <div class="question-mark">
          <span>Q:</span>
        </div>
        <div class="question-content">
```

```
            <h3 class="mb-0">{{question.title}}</h3>
          </div>
        </div>
        {% if request.user == question.author %}
        <div class="pl-2">
          <a href="{% url 'question_delete' question.pk %}" class="btn btn-sm btn-danger">
Delete</a>
        </div>
        {% endif %}
      </div>
    </div>
    <div class="row mt-5">
      <div class="col-12">
        <div class="question-detail-container">
          <div class="answers-container">
            <span id="answer-above"></span>
            <p class="loading-comment animate text-center">loading advices...</p>
            {% if request.user.is_authenticated %}
            <form class="post-answer-form">
              <div class="form-group">
                <label for="answer" class="answer-heading">Post an advice</label>
                <textarea class="form-control advice-form mb-2" name="answer" id="answer"
rows="5"></textarea>
                <button class="btn btn-primary" type="submit" id="post-
comment">Submit</button>
              </div>
              <p class="text-danger font-weight-bold" id="form-error"></p>
            </form>
            {% else %}
            <p class="answer-heading"><a href="{% url 'login' %}">Login</a> to post an
advice</p>
            {% endif %}
          </div>
        </div>
      </div>
    </div>
  </div>
{% endblock content %}
```

Code 84 financeblog\advice\templates\advice\question_detail.html

The template is the same as before except for a few changes. We have now added a form that allows users to post advice to the question. We have also added a floating message that says, "loading advice…".

Note that the form and the floating messages are pure HTML and CSS. We have yet to add any javascript to make them functional. Also, note that we are performing a check to see if the user is logged in or not and only then displaying the form. Take a look at our detail page (seen as guest).

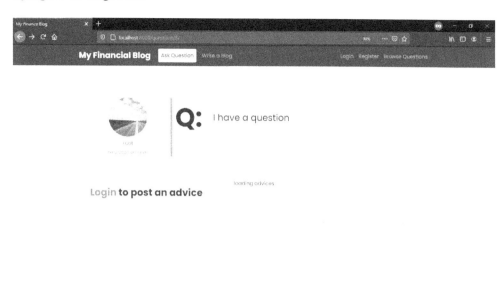

Figure 92 Question detail page when the user logged out

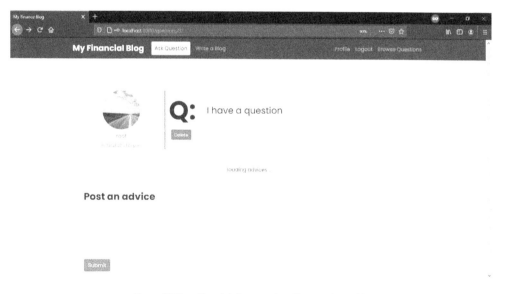

Figure 93 Question detail page when the user logged in

Let's add the javascript code to fetch this question's advice but first, let's open our **base.html** template and create a block template tag for js. Open the **base.html** template inside the **templates>blog** directory of the blog application and add the following code after the last script tag.

```
{% block js %}
{% endblock js %}
```

After making this change, your **base.html** template should have the rough structure of the following code snippet.

```
{% load static %}

        …

{% block content %}
{% endblock content %}

        …

    {% block js %}
    {% endblock js %}

  </body>
</html>
```

Code 85 financeblog\blog\templates\blog\base.html

The reason we are creating a new block template tag is that we will be using a Technology called **JQuery**. Since the content block comes before the script tags in the HTML document, our jquery code will throw errors because we are trying to use something that hasn't been loaded yet. Remember, HTML documents are read from top to bottom.

Now go back to the **question_detail.html** template and outside the content block and create a new **js** block. We are going to code a simple JS Method that will fetch data from our REST API and insert "live" into our HTML Page, that has **already** been loaded.

```
{% block js %}

<script>
$(document).ready(function(){
  // This function runs once and fetches the advices of this specific question.
  function fetchAdvicesUpdateUI(){

    // Fetching Data from our own REST API
    fetch("/questions/api/{{question.id}}")
    .then(res => res.json())
    .then(data => {
      let answers = []
      // Loop over the data returned from the api.
      for(var i = 0; i < data.length; i ++){

        // Constructing the markup from the data returned from API.
        var answer = [
          "<div class='answer'><div class='answer-by'>",
          "<a class='mugshot-container mb-1' href='",
          data[i].user_url,
          "'> <div class='mugshot-img-sm mb-2' style='background-image:url(",
          data[i].user_image,
          ")'></div><span>",
          data[i].username,
          "</span></a> <small class='text-muted'>",
          data[i].date_published,
          "</small></div><div class='answer-content'> <p>",
          data[i].content,
          "</p></div></div>"
        ]
        answers.push(answer.join(""))
      }

      if( answers.length < 1){
        answers = ['<p class="no-answer">No answers posted to this thread yet!</p>']
      } else{
        answers.unshift('<h3 class="answer-heading" id="answer-here">Answers:</h3>')
      }

      // Loop over the advices array and push it to our html document.
      for(var i = 0; i < answers.length; i++){
        $("#answer-above").before(answers[i])
      }

      // Hide the loading advices message.
      $(".loading-comment").css("display", "none")
  })
  }
  // Load the advices once on page was loaded.
  fetchAdvicesUpdateUI()
})
</script>

{% endblock js %}
```

Code 86 financeblog\advice\templates\advice\question_detail.html

This was much code so let's go over it in detail. We have opened the **js** block and have created a **script** tag inside it. We are using jquery's **ready** method to ensure that our code runs after the document has been fully loaded. Next, we have created a method called **fetchAdvicesUpdateUI** which will be responsible for calling the API and updating our page.

```
fetch("/questions/api/{{question.id}}")
.then(res => res.json())
.then(data => {...//other code}
```

This **fetch** function is a built-in javascript function used to make HTTP requests. We are requesting to "**/question/api/{{question.id}}**", **question.id** refers to the pk parameter our URL pattern expects. This will be used to identify which question's advice we need. This question will return us some sort of response, and we are retrieving our JSON data through that response.

Next, we are using that data to display the advice on our page. Note that we aren't passing a full path to the **fetch** method because when we pass partial paths like these, it assumes that we are talking about the current host.

We have heavily commented on the Jquery code to understand what it is doing. Still, just to give you the gist, after the API has returned the advice data, we are manipulating the HTML DOM and creating the structure of our advice. Next, we are adding that structure to the page and hiding the "**...loading advices**" message. Now when you open the detail page of a question, you should see its advice being fetched live.

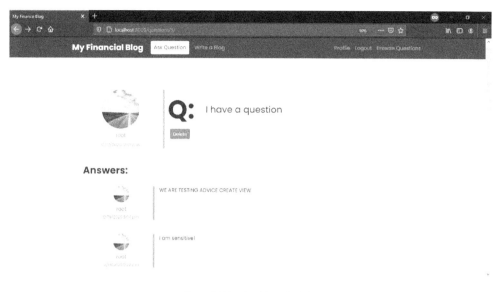

Figure 94 Live fetching of advice

CREATE ADVICE ON QUESTION DETAIL PAGE

Now that our advices are being fetched and we are displaying them successfully, it's time to set up our form so it sends data to the **AdviceCreateView** API and creates advice for us. Our **AdviceCreateView** API returns the newly created advice, and we will add that to our page.

Before we add the code, let's briefly talk about authentication. By default, Django uses session-based authentication. When we log in, the server creates a session, stores it in the database, and attaches a session id to the browser cookie. When we make further requests to the server, we send the session id with the request, and the server uses that to authenticate us. The HTTP protocol is stateless, meaning if we don't send the session cookie with the request, the server will not be able to recognize us and treat us as logged-out users.

We usually use Token Based authentication in the case of REST APIs, but for our use case where we will only be using the API on our web application through AJAX,

Django's default session authentication is more than enough for our current setup. Append the following javascript code to the script tag of the **question_detail.html** template.

```javascript
// Whenever form is submitted, execute following method.
$(".post-answer-form").on("submit", function (e) {
  e.preventDefault()
  // Pass the content from the input box
  postAdvice($('.advice-form').val())
})

function postAdvice(content) {
  // Check if answer was empty and return if true.
  if (content.length === 0) {
    $("#form-error").text("Can't be empty!")
    $("#form-error").css("display", "block")
    return;
  }
  $("#form-error").css("display", "none")
  // Hide button interaction
  $("#post-comment").text("Wait...").attr('disabled', true);

  // Construct data to send to our REST API
  var mydata = {
    'content': content,
  };

  // Insert question-id and user-token for the POST request.
  fetch('/questions/api/{{question.id}}/create', {
      method: 'POST',
      headers: {
        'Content-Type': 'application/json',
        // Get the csrf token.
        'X-CSRFTOKEN': Cookies.get('csrftoken')
      },
      // data we want to send to api
      body: JSON.stringify(mydata)
    })
    .then(res => res.json())
    .then(data => {

      // Constructing markup in array from data received.
      var answer = [
        "<div class='answer new-answer'><div class='answer-by'>",
        "<a class='mugshot-container mb-1' href='",
        data.user_url,
        "'> <div class='mugshot-img-sm mb-2' style='background-image:url(",
        data.user_image,
        ")'></div><span>",
        data.username,
        "</span></a> <small class='text-muted'>",
        data.date_published,
        "</small></div><div class='answer-content'> <p>",
        data.content,
        "</p></div></div>"
      ]

      // If answers exist, post before the latest answer (at the top).
      if ($(".answer").length > 0) {
        $("#answer-here").after(answer.join(''));
      } else {
```

```
            // If this is the first anser, this will be posted before the identifier.
        $("#answer-above").after('<h3 class="answer-heading" id="answer-
here">Answers:</h3>')
        $("#answer-here").after(answer.join(''))
        $(".no-answer").css("display", "none")
      }
      // Updating button to 'clickable' and changing text back to "Submit".
      $("#post-comment").text("Submit").attr('disabled', false);
      // Clear the input field.
      $('.advice-form').val("");
      // Scroll to answer we just saved and the api returned.
      $("html, body").animate({
        scrollTop: $("#answer-here").offset().top
      }, 500);
      // Unfocus the submit button.
      $("#post-comment").blur();
    })
    .catch(err => console.log(err))
}
```

Code 87 financeblog\advice\templates\advice\question_detail.html

We have prevented the default behaviour of the form on submit and are running a function called **postAdvice**. To **postAdvice** we are passing the contents of the text area where the user entered their advice.

After performing some checks on the user-submitted data, we are storing it in an object **my_data** under the critical **content**. If you remember, our API only expects a **content** field. This is where the magic happens.

```
fetch('/questions/api/{{question.id}}/create', {
  method: 'POST',
  headers: {
    'Content-Type': 'application/json',
    // we get the csrf token and attach it to our request
    'X-CSRFTOKEN': Cookies.get('csrftoken')
  },
              // data we want to send to api
  body: JSON.stringify(mydata)
})
.then(res => res.json())
.then(data => {//...other code}
```

This piece of JS Code sends a POST-Request to the REST API path "**/questions/api/{{question.pk}}/create**". Inside the headers, we are telling the

Backend that our Request Body we will be of type JSON. We have to pass the **csrftoken** to identify ourself, and it'll be used to authenticate the incoming request at the view.

We are fetching the **csrftoken** from the browser using the cookies library we imported in our **base.html** in the second chapter. Remember, this cookie was sent to our browser by the Server (Django). Lastly, we are attaching our **my_data** object after converting it to JSON string into the request's body.

When we perform the request, the API will return the newly created advice instance to us, and we are then handling that data to display the advice on the page. You can read the comments of the code to see how we are displaying the returned data.

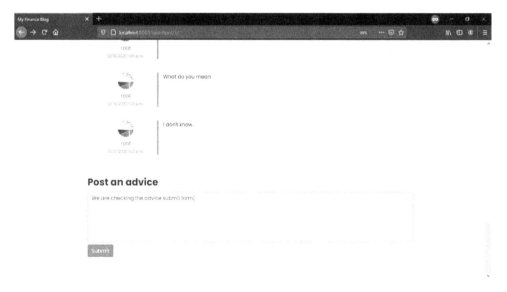

Figure 95 Advice submitting

Upon pressing the submit button, you will be taken to the top of the page, and your newly created advice will be shown to you in a nice animation.

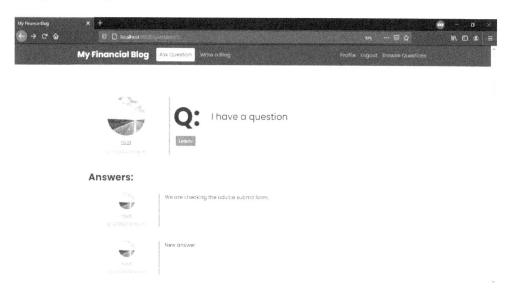

Figure 96 Newly created advice view

Submitting an empty advice, will return an error. As we can see, our advices are getting saved successfully and we can see them appear on the page without the page even reloading. Your **question_detail.html** template should look like this after adding the js for the list and create API.

```
{% extends "blog/base.html" %}

{% block content %}
...
{% endblock content %}

{% block js %}
<script>
  $(document).ready(function () {
    function fetchAdvicesUpdateUI() {
      ...
    }
    //Load the advices once on page load.
    fetchAdvicesUpdateUI()

    //whenever form is submitted, we run this function.
    $(".post-answer-form").on("submit", function (e) {
      ...
    })

    function postAdvice(content) {
      ...
    }
  })
</script>
{% endblock js %}
```

Code 88 financeblog\advice\templates\advice\question_detail.html

That is it. You've been exposed to a pretty wide (but still deep) set of tools in the Django Universe. The next thing we will do is show our Application to the world. Sell you App, your Idea, your Product, or whatever it is that you will be developing with Django 3.

CLOUD DEPLOY

WHAT IS SERVERLESS DEPLOYMENT?

In a traditional hosting strategy, we buy a hosting from a hosting service provider, which is usually a linux machine. We then have to configure it ourselves to run our application. For example we have to install python, django, manage proxies and load balancers etc. Also note that we get a fixed amount of resources(RAM, CPU) core in the hosting package that we buy.

This model has a few problems. First is that you have to pay a fixed amount no matter if the work you are doing doesn't justify the costs at all. Second is it gets harder if we want to scale the application. A sudden increase in traffic or the like can very likely shut down your server unless you upgrade your hosting plan.

With serverless, we don't have to manage the servers ourselves. All we do is that we deploy our code and the serverless service provider manages it for us. Do note that there are still servers involved, it's just that managing them have been abstracted away from us. One more plus point of a serverless hosting is that you only pay for the amount of time your application is ran. The actual specifics are different but the idea is generally the same. For example, one serverless service provider might charge you based per request made to the server or others might charge you some minuscle amount of money for every GB of memory used etc.

That is why, for this guide, we will deploy our application to a serverless hosting.

GOOGLE CLOUD RUN + DOCKER

We will be using Google Cloud run for this purpose as well as docker. We'll use a variety of backing services with google cloud run to ensure our application works correctly. Which backing services you might ask? Google cloud run will only store and run your code. You still need a database to save the data as well as some sort of space to store static files(css files, js files and user uploaded images etc).

For these purposes we will use Google cloud SQL and Google Cloud storage. You can sign up for Google Cloud run and you will get $300 in credit free when you provide your billing credentials. Don't worry as you'll not be charged, this is just so they can keep spam at low. This free tier is good enough for development and testing purposes so we will go with it.

WHAT IS DOCKER?

You might be wondering what Docker is. Docker is a way to sort of containerize your application so it behaves the same way no matter which os and machine you run it on.

In simple terms, Suppose you are working on a django application on a linux machine with some version of python. Your friend wants to help with your code but they are running a windows machine with a different python version. Some problems might occur as you both try to run the same code and you might get around it by using virtualenvs but it's still very prone to error and bugs.

Enter Docker. Docker will put all of your code in a container (think of it as a virtual environment) and you can run it pretty much on any machine that has docker installed on it. It doesn't matter whether the other machine has python or not, docker will internally take care of everything and reproduce the same environment on each machine so the application behaves as expected.

> *Think of Docker as Virtual Machines - but lightweight and fast as compared to a virtual machine.*

INSTALLING DOCKER

If you haven't installed Docker for the PostgreSQL Database, you will need to do it now. Head over to https://www.docker.com/products/docker-desktop and download Docker Desktop. You should choose the version for your OS. The installation process will be mostly the same. After downloading and opening the setup file.

It will download some packages and then ask for these components. The first one is compulsory so check it and proceed to clicking the ok button. If you're on windows, you'll probably get the following error while restarting after the setup completes.

Since Windows doesn't have a linux kernel by default, this error is understandable. Follow the link, install all necessary dependencies and return.

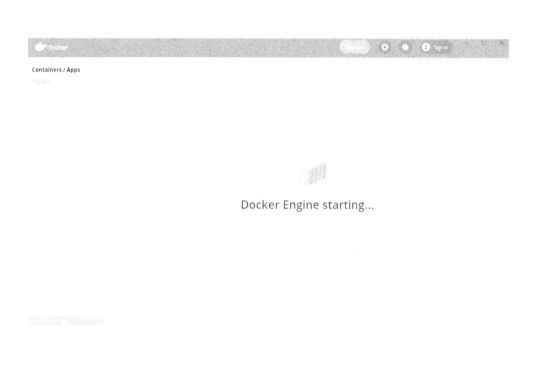

SETTING UP GOOGLE CLOUD

With docker installed, we need to configure the backing services we'll need to run our project on google cloud run. First, head over to google cloud console at https://console.cloud.google.com. If this is your first time opening cloud console, you'll probably be shown a welcome screen.

Select their terms of service and continue. Next you should enable billing for your cloud console by clcking the "Activate" button at the top right side of the screen. As stated before, you'll get $300 in credit which is more than enough for our blogging application just for testing purposes. If in th future this $300 credit does run out, google will prompt you to manually continute to paying for services instead of automatically deducting money from your account which is a big plus.

SETTING UP A GOOGLE CLOUD PROJECT

With billing enabled, you now need to create a new project on the cloud console. Click the "Select a project" link on the nav bar on the home screen of google cloud console.

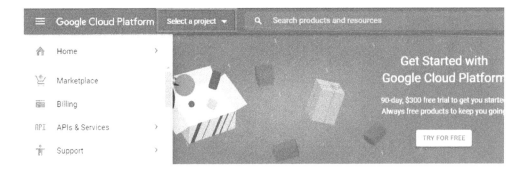

New Project

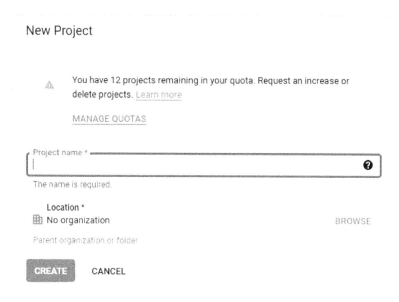

Under Project name, enter a name for your project and keep the Location option as default. After creating the project, you'll be redirected to the Google Cloud Dashboard.

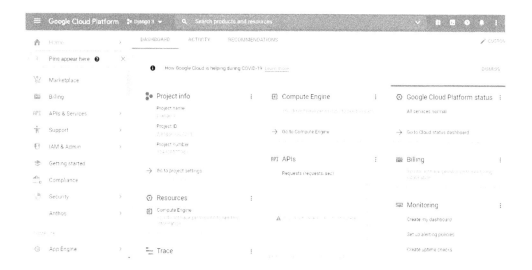

Great, your google cloud project has been created. If you can see, I called my project "Django 3". There is also a field called **Project ID**. **Please keep this field in mind as we'll use it to identify this project when creating the backing services.**

INSTALLING CLOUD SDK

We'll need google cloud sdk to be able to interact with cloud console from our machine. Head over to https://cloud.google.com/sdk/docs/install and download the version for your os. Since I'm on a windows machine, I'll download the windows version.

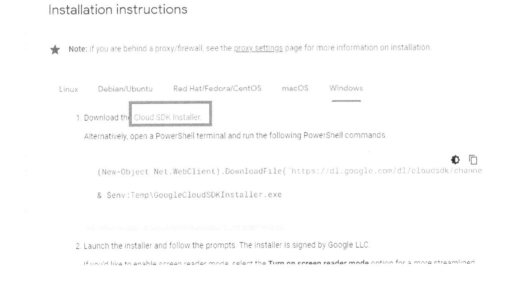

After downloading the setup, run the installer and click yourself through it...you know the drill.

If everything worked, you should see a prompt that will ask you log in into your Google Cloud Account or Project.

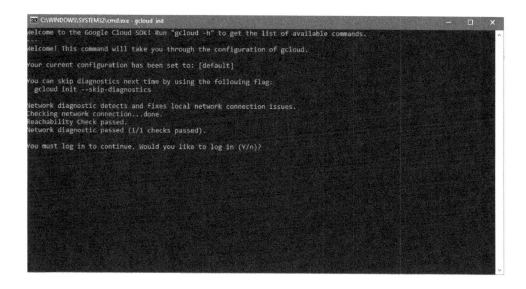

Enter "y" and you'll be redirected to your browser for authentication purposes. Enter your credentials and you'll be asked to provide permissions to cloud sdk.

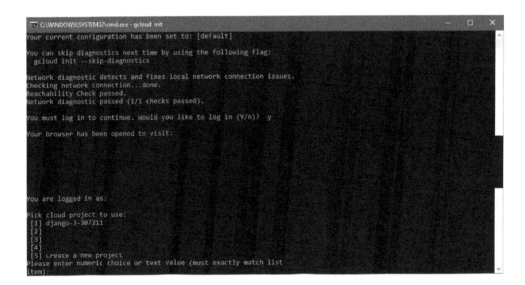

As you can see, my project django-3 is showing here. Since my project is at number "1", I'll enter that into the command prompt.

SETTING UP CLOUDSQL

Our django application uses a PostgresSql database. Remember, Cloud run just runs our code, we still need a database separate from cloud run. We'll use Google's CloudSQL. In your cloud console dashboard in your current project, search for Google Cloud SQL.

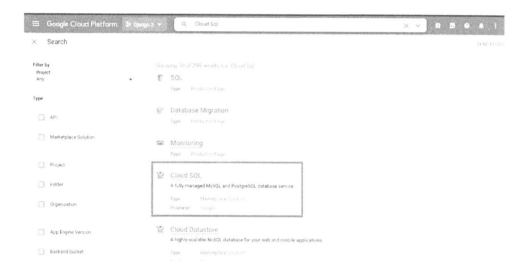

Select "GO TO CLOUD SQL" and you'll be redirected to another screen where you'll be asked to create a new instance. Make sure you are on the right project by looking at the drop down next to "Google Cloud Platform" link in the header. When you click "CREATE INSTANCE", you'll be taken to another screen.

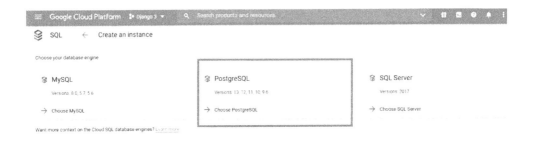

Since our Django 3 Application uses PostgresSQL database, we'll select PostgresSQL instance.

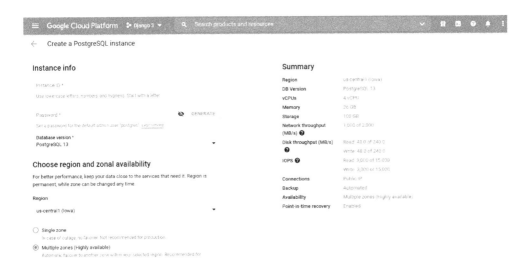

You'll then be taken to a form for creating a PostgresSql instance. Note that we are not creating a "database" yet, this is sort of like installing PostgresSql on your machine.

In the "**Instance ID**" field, enter a name you want to use for this instance. I'm calling mine "**django-3-postgres-instance**". The password field is for the default "**postgres**" user. Make sure that the password is a strong one. Leave all other fields as they are and click create instance. If your instance was created successfully, you'll be redirected to the following page

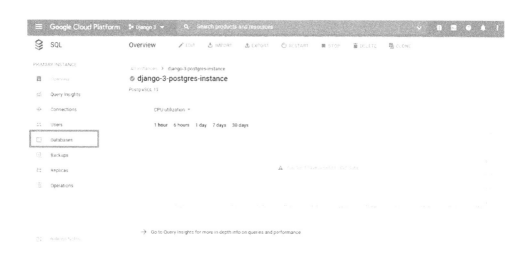

Next click the "**Databases**" link on the side navigation bar and you'll be taken to a new page.

Create a new database by clicking the "**CREATE DATABSE**" button. You'll be prompted to select a name for your database. I'm calling my database "**django-3-postgres-database**". After creating your database successfully, you'll now see your newly created database listed here.

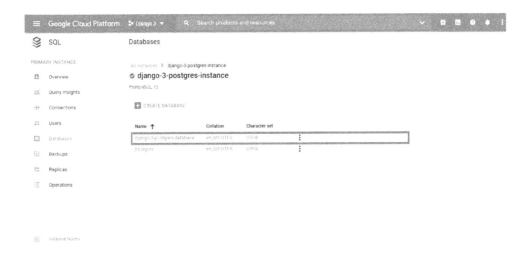

Next we need to create a **User** for our database. We'll do this from the coud console online shell. On your navigation bar at the top, there should be a console icon on the right side

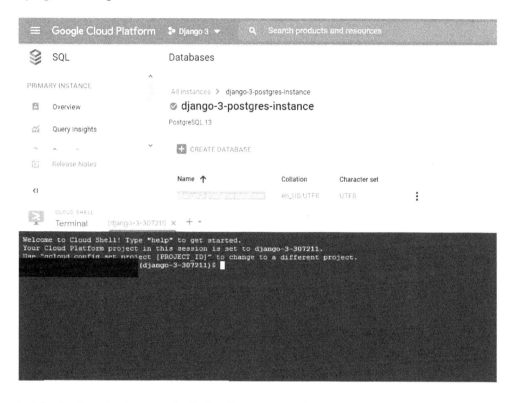

Inside the Terminal, enter the following command:

```
gcloud sql connect <your cloudsqlinstance name> --user postgres
```

Do note that you are to enter you instance name, not your database name. We are creating a new user on our postgres instance. My instance name is **django-3-postgres-instance** so my command will become.

```
gcloud sql connect django-3-postgres-instance --user postgres
```

You might be asked to enter your google credentials. Afterwards, you'll be asked to enter the password for the "**postgres**" superuser of your database instance. Enter the password for your **postgres** user that you chose previously while creating the PostgresSql instance and you'll be given access to the **PostgresSql** shell as shown in the image below.

```
Welcome to Cloud Shell! Type "help" to get started.
Your Cloud Platform project in this session is set to django-3-307211.
Use "gcloud config set project [PROJECT_ID]" to change to a different project.
                        ~ (django-3-307211)$ gcloud sql connect django-3-postgres-instance --user postgres
Allowlisting your IP for incoming connection for 5 minutes...#

Allowlisting your IP for incoming connection for 5 minutes...done.
Connecting to database with SQL user [postgres].Password:
psql (13.2 (Debian 13.2-1.pgdg100+1), server 13.1)
SSL connection (protocol: TLSv1.3, cipher: TLS_AES_256_GCM_SHA384, bits: 256, compression: off)
Type "help" for help.

postgres=> ▮
```

Once you have access to the postgres shell, run the following command to create a new user called Django.

```
CREATE USER test WITH PASSWORD 'your_password_here';
```

Make sure you replace the above string with your password. I've named this user **test,** you can call it whatever you want. Finally, give this user all rights on your database by running the following command.

```
GRANT ALL PRIVILEGES ON DATABASE '<your_database_name>' TO test
```

Do note that we are now referencing the database name, not our PostgresSql installation instance name. I named my database '**django-3-postgres-database**'. Here's the shell output. Great, Our postgres database is ready to be utilized.

CLOUD STORAGE BUCKET

Our database setup is complete. We now need to set up Cloud Storage bucket which will hold all of our static files and user uploaded images. A bucket is sort of a directory where you will store all of your files. We'll be storing all the django static files inside a such bucket.

As for why we need a separate place for storing static files, If you remember, way earlier in the tutorial, django is not suitable for serving static assets. Moreover, cloud run will only run the code and not store any files we upload to a storage. That is where Cloud Storage comes into picture. There are other options such as Amazon s3 buckets but we'll use Google's Cloud Storage.

Head over to https://console.cloud.google.com/storage/browser. Click the "Create Bucket" button to create a new bucket. Follow the steps described in the images attached below.

← Create a bucket

- **Name your bucket**

  Pick a **globally unique**, permanent name. Naming guidelines

  django-3-bucket

  Tip: Don't include any sensitive information

  CONTINUE

- **Choose where to store your data**

- **Choose a default storage class for your data**

- **Choose how to control access to objects**

- **Advanced settings (optional)**

  CREATE   CANCEL

✓ **Name your bucket**

- **Choose where to store your data**

  This permanent choice defines the geographic placement of your data and affects
  cost, performance, and availability. Learn more

  Location type

  ○ Region
    Lowest latency within a single region

  ○ Dual-region
    High availability and low latency across 2 regions

  ⦿ Multi-region
    Highest availability across largest area

  Location

  us (multiple regions in United States)   ▼

  CONTINUE

✔ **Name your bucket**

✔ **Choose where to store your data**

• **Choose a default storage class for your data**

A storage class sets costs for storage, retrieval, and operations. Pick a default
storage class based on how long you plan to store your data and how often it will
be accessed. Learn more

◉ Standard ❓
  Best for short-term storage and frequently accessed data

◯ Nearline
  Best for backups and data accessed less than once a month

◯ Coldline
  Best for disaster recovery and data accessed less than once a quarter

◯ Archive
  Best for long-term digital preservation of data accessed less than once a year

CONTINUE

• **Choose how to control access to objects**

Give your bucket a unique name. I've called my bucket "**django-3-bucket**".Choose
Fine-Grained as access control. I've left other fields as default but I've still shown
them in the images attached just to avoid any confusions. If everything goes okay,
you'll be redirected to the following screen

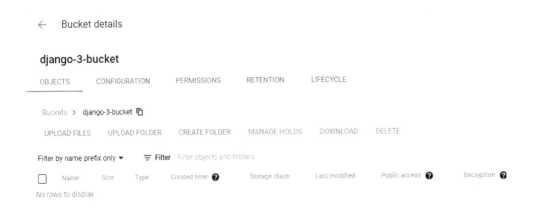

INFORMATION IN SECRET MANAGER

We are finished setting the backing services. We'll use these services in our django project but linking them in our settings.py file is a serious security flaw as it'll be visible. We need to store the information regarding these services inside a secret environment. Google Cloud's Secret Manager is the tool for this purpose.

First, create a file called **.env** somewhere on your computer. Open it with a code editor and add the following strings to it:

```
DATABASE_URL=postgres://<db_user_you_created>:<password_of_the_db_user>@//cloudsql/<your_p
roject_id>:<region_of_the_db>:<db_instance_name>/<db_name>
GS_BUCKET_NAME=<your bucket name>
SECRET_KEY=<just enter a random key here...>
```

You have to enter your data in the bolded text fields. First we are defining a key called DATABASE_URL. We'll use this inside our django project to connect to the database we just created on cloud console. In case you are confused as to what **"<your_project_id>:<region_of_the_db>:<db_instance_name>/<db_name>"** mean, this is the connection string used to identify the database you created earlier.

If you have trouble recalling the names of the database and instance name of cloud sql, simply head over to https://console.cloud.google.com/sql/instances/, and you will see the database you created earlier listed over there. Click your instance and you'll be taken to it's detail page. After scrolling down a bit, you should see "Connection String".

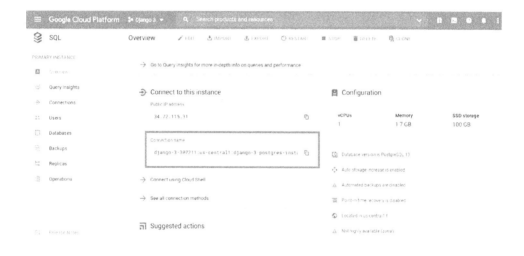

Copy this connection string and put it into the DATABASE_URL key.Note that this is your sql instance connection string. You you have to append your database name to the end of this connection string. Also note to add the database user and the database user's password to the key. My DATABASE_URL key will look like this.

```
DATABASE_URL=postgres://test:my_user_password_here@//cloudsql/django-3-307211:us-
central1:django-3-postgres-instance/django-3-postgres-database
```

The **GS_BUCKET_NAME** is simple, you just need to append the name of the cloud storage buket you created earlier. If you don't remember your bucket name, you can refer to it by navigating to the cloud storage page inside cloud console.

Lastly, in the SECRET_KEY key, enter a random generated string of length 50. You can generate a secret key by entering numbers manually or using a generator like https://miniwebtool.com/django-secret-key-generator/.

After you are finished entering correct data into the **.env** file, head over to https://console.cloud.google.com/security/secret-manager and create a new secret (make sure you are on the correct project by checking th top navigation bar). When you create a new secret, You'll be redirected to a new form.

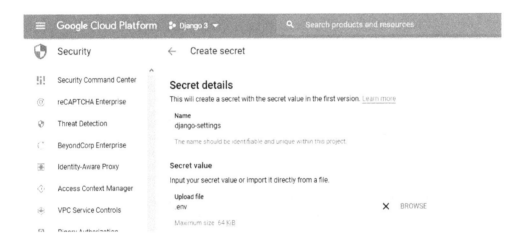

Give it the name "**django-settings**" and upload the **.env** file we just created. Leave other fields as they are and create the secret. You will then be redirected to the detail page of the secret you just created.

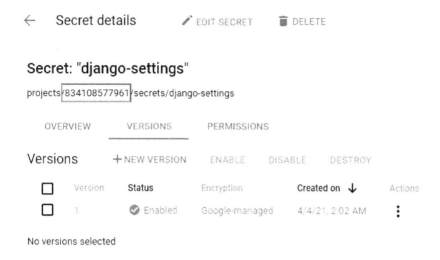

Note the highlighted secretid in the image attached below as we'll be using it later. It is under **projects/<secretid>/secrets/django-settings**. Next select the **Permission** tab on the same page and click "Add Member".

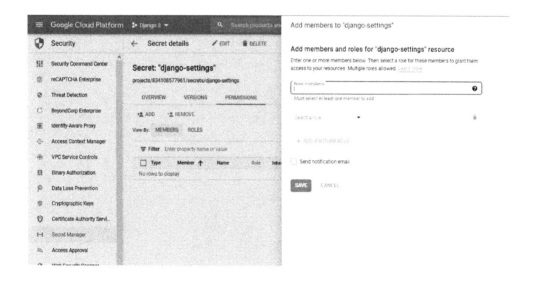

In the "New Members" field, using the **<secretid>** we copied in the step before, add the following two strings:

```
<secretid>-compute@developer.gserviceaccount.com
<secretid>@cloudbuild.gserviceaccount.com
```

Filling the placeholders with my data I get:

```
834108577961-compute@developer.gserviceaccount.com
834108577961@cloudbuild.gserviceaccount.com
```

From the roles dropdown, select **Secret Ma`nager Secret Accessor** and hit save.

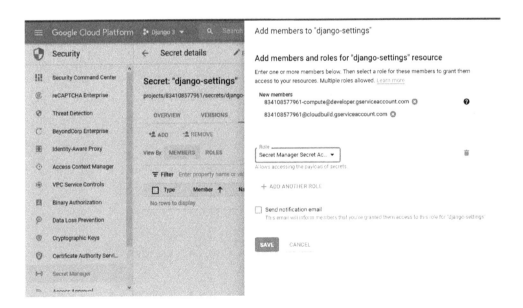

Django 3 for Beginners

Go back to secret manager page and create a new secret called "superuser_password". This secret will basically act as the password of the django website superuser in production deployment. Keep this in mind as you'll be using it to logn to the admin panel of our website. In the value field, set a password for the user:

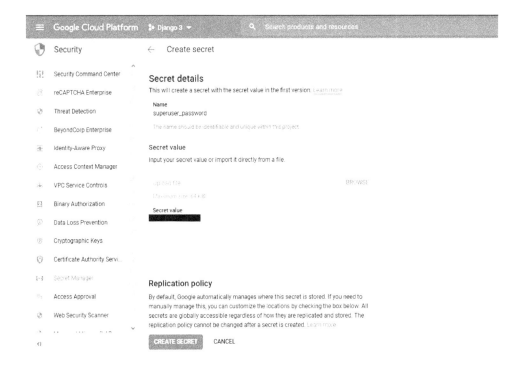

Just like we did with the last secret, go to the permissions tab and select Add members. Add only the following string in the New members field:

```
<secretid>@cloudbuild.gserviceaccount.com
```

Next, select the **Secret Manager Secret Accessor** as the role just like we did previously. Finally, save and your secrets are ready. Let's talk about why we created a secret for super user password. We usually create the superuser through the django terminal but in deployment, we'll be creating it with a migration file. We'll pull the password from the environment dynamically and create the user. You'll see what it means in a bit.

CLOUD BUILD ACCESS TO CLOUD SQL

Our cloud build will need to run the database migrations but it doesn't have access to it by default. Let's give it appropriate access. Head over to https://console.cloud.google.com/iam-admin/iam and again, make sure you are under the correct project. You'll be taken to a screen like so.

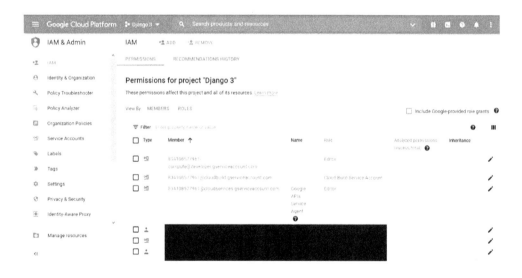

In the previos step when creating secret manager for django settings and admin password, I asked you to hold on to the **secretid**. It's this one if you don't remember and it is visible on your secret manager page.

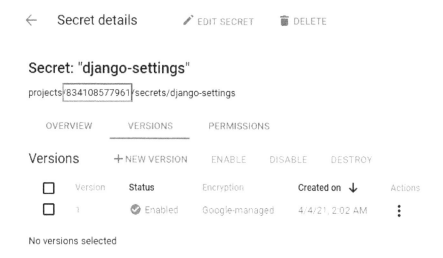

Now on the current page, "IAM & ADMIN" page that you are on, you want to search for "**<yoursecretid>@cloudbuild.gserviceaccount.com**", in my case, it becomes: **834108577961@cloudbuild.gserviceaccount.com** as you can see on my screen (note: your id will be different from mine).

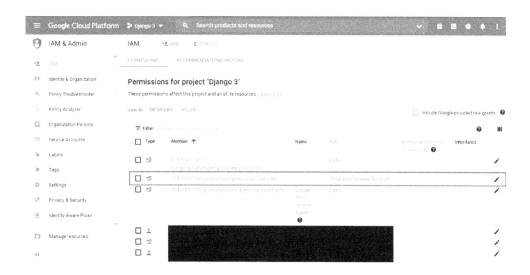

Click the edit "pencil" button next to the highlighted account and the following sidebar will open.Click the "ADD ANOTHER ROLE" button and select "Cloud SQL Client". Click save and exit.

PREPARING CODE FOR DEPLOYMENT

Now that our backing services have been configured, we can deploy our django application to the web. However we need to make adjustments to our code and make it ready for deployment.

For example, we need to configure the project to store and get static assets from Cloud Storage, save data to Cloud sql etc. Also note that we will be starting from a new and empty database. This means that whatever redundant data we have on our local database, will not make it to the production environment. We also suggest you to create a copy of your project in case anything goes wrong.

INSTALLING MODULES

Google cloud run will need a way to know which python modules our project uses. For that, we will create a file called requirements.txt and put all of the modules required by our application inside that file. Go to the root of your project's directory and run the following command(make sure your virtual env is running).

```
(MyProject) E:\MyProject\financeblog>pip freeze > requirements.txt
```

Running the above command should have created a file called **requirements.txt** in the root of your project directory. If you've followed the tutorial so far, the **requirements.txt** file will have the following content (versions might differ).

```
asgiref==3.3.1
Django==3.1.3
django-cors-headers==3.6.0
django-crispy-forms==1.10.0
djangorestframework==3.12.2
djangorestframework-simplejwt==4.6.0
Markdown==3.3.3
Pillow==8.0.1
psycopg2==2.8.6
PyJWT==2.0.0
pytz==2020.4
sqlparse==0.4.1
```

For our production environment, we will need a few more python modules e.g django-storages for connecting to the Cloud Storage, django-environs for managing environment variables etc. Add the following new modules to our **requirements.txt** file so it looks like this.

```
gunicorn==20.0.4
psycopg2-binary==2.8.5
google-cloud-secret-manager==2.1.0
google-auth==1.24.0
django-storages[google]==1.9.1
django-environ==0.4.5
```

We've removed one module i.e. psycopg2, which we were using to connect to our local database. Our cloud version woud not be needing this module.

CREATING SUPER USER

Since we will be starting from an empty database, we will not have our superuser on the produciton version by default, we will have to create one. However it will be very difficult to open a terminal in the context of our running application once it is on the cloud. Therefore we will not be able to create a django superuser the normal way i.e. by running the createsuperuser command.

We will use a technique called data migration. It is a way of making changes to the database (these can be CRUD operations) by regular migration files. If you remember, Django creates a migration file for each of the Model we define or make changes to and when we run our migrations, those schema changes get updated to the database. A data migration is similar but we have to create the migration file ourselves and it will make changes to the data inside the database.

CREATING DATA MIGRATION FOR SUPERUSER

If we create a migration file in one of our existing applications, it can cause conflicts with the existing Django migration files of that specific application, that is why, we will create a new application. Head over to the root directory of your project and create a new application by running the following command.

```
(MyProject) E:\MyProject\financeblog>python manage.py startapp superuser
```

This command will create a new application called superuser in your project. This application will have no functionality, we will only be using it to create our data migration. As stated before, if we were to create a data migration in one of our existing applications, it would clash with one of the existing migrations and while those are solvable, they are very hard to debug. That is why we are choosing this simple approach. Next head over to the **settings.py** located inside your project's directory under the path.

Add the application we just created to the **settings.py** where our other applications are listed.

```
INSTALLED_APPS = [
    'django.contrib.admin',
    'django.contrib.auth',
    'django.contrib.contenttypes',
    'django.contrib.sessions',
    'django.contrib.messages',
    'django.contrib.staticfiles',
    'blog',
    'profiles',
    'crispy_forms',
    'advice',
    'rest_framework',
    'superuser' # <-new app here
]
```

Now that our application is registered, we can create the data migration file by running the following command.

```
(MyProject) E:\MyProject\financeblog>manage.py makemigrations --empty superuser
Migrations for 'superuser':
  superuser\migrations\0001_initial.py
```

This command will create a data migration file for us inside our **superuser** application. Open the newly created file in your **superuser** application directory.

Override the contents of the file with the following code.

```
from django.db import migrations

import google.auth
from google.cloud import secretmanager as sm

def createsuperuser(apps, schema_editor):

    # Retrieve secret from Secret Manager
    project_id = "django-3-307211"
    _, project = google.auth.default()
    client = sm.SecretManagerServiceClient()
    admin_password = client.access_secret_version(request={"name": "projects/"+project_id+
"/secrets/superuser_password/versions/1"}).payload.data.decode("UTF-8")

    # Create a new user using acquired password
    from django.contrib.auth.models import User
    User.objects.create_superuser("admin", password=admin_password)

class Migration(migrations.Migration):

    initial = True

    dependencies = [
    ]

    operations = [
        migrations.RunPython(createsuperuser)
    ]
```

The code is a bit complicated but we will simplify it for you. The only important part of this code is this.

```
    # Retrieve secret from Secret Manager
    project_id = "django-3-307211"
    _, project = google.auth.default()
    client = sm.SecretManagerServiceClient()
    admin_password = client.access_secret_version(request={"name": "projects/"+project_id+
"/secrets/superuser_password/versions/1"}).payload.data.decode("UTF-8")

    # Create a new user using acquired password
    from django.contrib.auth.models import User
    User.objects.create_superuser("admin", password=admin_password)
```

Since our project will be ran in the cloud, we will have access to our project by using the googl auth module. We are retrieving the current project and then using that project's name, we are pulling the **admin_password** secret we created earlier in our secret manager. Also note that in the **project_id** variable, you have to put your cloud console project id. Mine is **django-3-307211** so i've used that. We don't have to authenticate ourselves here, as this code will be executed in the "**Cloud Run**" Service where we will already be authenticated.

In short, In this file we are using the google cloud serect manager module to retrieve our password that we stored earlier in our Google Secret Manager and used it to create a new superuser.

Now whenever we run our migrations, Django will look at this migration file and create a superuser with the password supplied by the secret manager. Of course it will give us error as our code is right now so let's move on to adjusting our code.

CONFIGURING THE SETTINGS.PY FILE

We need to configure our project settings. For example, we are currently storing static and media files in our local storage using the "**STATIC_URL**" and "**MEDIA_URL**" settings. We need to remove these and configure the project so it uses the Cloud storage. We also need to import the secret manager **.env** file that we uploaded to google secret manager earlier. We will get the connection string for the db from the env file.

You know the drill, head over to the **settings.py** file of our project. Before proceeding further, if you haven't already created a backup of the project, at least create a backup of the settings.py file. This file will undergo, as you might expect, the thoughest surgery. Before we dive into the details of what needs to be changed, here is the final fully functional settings.py.

```
from pathlib import Path
import io
import environ
import google.auth
from google.cloud import secretmanager

#create instance of environment variable
```

```python
env = environ.Env()
#retrieve current project from google cloud
_, project = google.auth.default()
# name of the secret manager where we uploaded our .env file
SETTINGS_NAME = "django_settings"
#creating instance of secret manager to pull secrets from
client = secretmanager.SecretManagerServiceClient()
project_id = "django-3-307211"
payload = client.access_secret_version(request={"name": "projects/"+project_id+"/secrets/d
jango-settings/versions/1"}).payload.data.decode("UTF-8")
# load secret manager data into environment variable
env.read_env(io.StringIO(payload))

BASE_DIR = Path(__file__).resolve().parent.parent
SECRET_KEY = env("SECRET_KEY")
DEBUG = False
ALLOWED_HOSTS = ["*"]
INSTALLED_APPS = [
    'django.contrib.admin',
    'django.contrib.auth',
    'django.contrib.contenttypes',
    'django.contrib.sessions',
    'django.contrib.messages',
    'django.contrib.staticfiles',
    'blog',
    'profiles',
    'crispy_forms',
    'advice',
    'rest_framework',
    'superuser',
    'storages'
]

MIDDLEWARE = [
    'django.middleware.security.SecurityMiddleware',
    'django.contrib.sessions.middleware.SessionMiddleware',
    'django.middleware.common.CommonMiddleware',
    'django.middleware.csrf.CsrfViewMiddleware',
    'django.contrib.auth.middleware.AuthenticationMiddleware',
    'django.contrib.messages.middleware.MessageMiddleware',
    'django.middleware.clickjacking.XFrameOptionsMiddleware',
]
ROOT_URLCONF = 'financeblog.urls'
TEMPLATES = [
    {
        'BACKEND': 'django.template.backends.django.DjangoTemplates',
        'DIRS': [],
        'APP_DIRS': True,
        'OPTIONS': {
            'context_processors': [
                'django.template.context_processors.debug',
                'django.template.context_processors.request',
                'django.contrib.auth.context_processors.auth',
                'django.contrib.messages.context_processors.messages',
            ],
        },
    },
]

WSGI_APPLICATION = 'financeblog.wsgi.application'
DATABASES = {"default": env.db()}

...

#responsible for pulling the cloud storage bucket name
GS_BUCKET_NAME = env("GS_BUCKET_NAME")
```

```
# setting the default storage of our django to cloud storage
DEFAULT_FILE_STORAGE = "storages.backends.gcloud.GoogleCloudStorage"
# setting cloud storage as default for putting static asset
STATICFILES_STORAGE = "storages.backends.gcloud.GoogleCloudStorage"
# making files available to public view
GS_DEFAULT_ACL = "publicRead"
```

We haven't changed the file too much – but these changes are make-or-brake type of changes for the Cloud Deployment. We have added explanation comments at the part that changed. Let's look at the part where we added new code and chaned previuos code.

```
import io
import environ
import google.auth
from google.cloud import secretmanager
```

Here we are importing a module called environ(package is django-environ). We will be using the module for creating environment variables. Speaking of environment variables, we will be pulling these from our Google Secret Manager using the google.auth and google.cloud modules.

```
#create instance of environment variable
env = environ.Env()
#retrieve current project from google cloud
_, project = google.auth.default()
# name of the secret manager where we uploaded our .env file
SETTINGS_NAME = "django_settings"
#creating instance of secret manager to pull secrets from
client = secretmanager.SecretManagerServiceClient()
project_id = "django-3-307211"
payload = client.access_secret_version(request={"name": "projects/"+project_id+"/secrets/d
jango-settings/versions/1"}).payload.data.decode("UTF-8")
# load secret manager data into environment variable
env.read_env(io.StringIO(payload))
```

In this piece of code, we are first creating an instance of the environ module. Next we are fetching the google cloud project from the google auth module. How does it know which project we are talking about? It will know this because this code will be deployed to a specific cloud project i.e. django-3 google cloud project in my case.

If you remember, we called our secret manager which holds our env file, "**django_settings**". We are using this name to pull the **.env** file from our Secret Manager and feeding it to the environment variable we created earlier. As we stated before, note the connection string, you have to pass your project id.

```
SECRET_KEY = env("SECRET_KEY")
```

We are now pulling the secret key from our environment variable. It gets this from the secret manager it pulled in the previos step.

```
DEBUG = False
```

We have also set debug to false so error messages aren't logged on the screens of the users browsing our website.

```
ALLOWED_HOSTS = ["*"]
```

In **ALLOWED_HOSTS** setting, we have set the asterik character which basically means to allow access from any url. Since we want the whole world to be able to browse our website, we used this setting.

```
INSTALLED_APPS = [
    'django.contrib.admin',
    'django.contrib.auth',
    'django.contrib.contenttypes',
    'django.contrib.sessions',
    'django.contrib.messages',
    'django.contrib.staticfiles',
    'blog',
    'profiles',
    'crispy_forms',
    'advice',
    'rest_framework',
    'superuser' ,
    'storages'
]
```

We have added an app called "**storages**" to our list of installed apps. This application will be responsible for letting us communicate with Cloud Storage.

```
DATABASES = {"default": env.db()}
```

In our databases setting, we are pulling the connection string from our environment variable. If you remember, we added the connection string to the .env file before we saved it to the Secret Manager. The **.db()** method automatically fetches any database settings we have on our environment variable. We could have simply stated **env("DATABASE_URL")** as we did with pulling the secret key, but this is the preferred method.

```
#responsible for pulling the cloud storage bucket name
GS_BUCKET_NAME = env("GS_BUCKET_NAME")
# setting the default storage of our django to cloud storage
DEFAULT_FILE_STORAGE = "storages.backends.gcloud.GoogleCloudStorage"
# setting cloud storage as default for putting static asset
STATICFILES_STORAGE = "storages.backends.gcloud.GoogleCloudStorage"
# making files available to public view
GS_DEFAULT_ACL = "publicRead"
```

We are getting our cloud storage bucket name from the environment variable. Next we are setting the default static assets storage as well as the storage for media files so it uses Cloud Storage bucket. Lastly, we are making the files stored on Cloud Storage bucket accessible to the public internet as we want users to be able to view media files and use our static assets (css, and js files).

If you noticed, we removed the "**STATIC_URL**","**MEDIA_URL**" and "**MEDIA_ROOT**" as those settings used local storage for storing media and asset files. These are all the changes we've made to the code.

CHANGING IMAGE URLS IN OUR REST APIS

Currently, the url links of the images returned in our REST APIs of the Advice application are not configured for production. That is because by default when using local storage, DRF(Django rest framework) only returns the relative path of media files, not the absolute path. A path to an image looks like "/media/image1.jpg".

That is why we have appended the name of the domain before this string and then we returned the response. This was good in development but since we are now using storage buckets, DRF will return full absolute url paths. We have to adjust the current code. Head over to the **views.py** file found inside **advice>views.py**. At line 33, we have the following code.

```
"user_image":request.build_absolute_uri(advice.author.profile.image.url),
```

Change it to:

```
"user_image":advice.author.profile.image.url,
```

At line 51, we have the previous same code:

320

```
"user_image":request.build_absolute_uri(advice.author.profile.image.url),
```

Again, change it to:

```
user_image = advice.author.profile.image.url
```

As you can see, before we were building the full image path ourselves, but now we are simply returning the path returned by django as it'll be a full path to where the images will be stored on storage bucket.

CONTAINERIZING THE PROJECT

As we stated before, in google cloud run, Docker containers are run. We need to containarize our project. In the root of your project, create a file called **Dockerfile**. Add the following code to it.

```
FROM python:3.8-slim

ENV APP_HOME /app
WORKDIR $APP_HOME

#better loggin
ENV PYTHONUNBUFFERED 1

# Install modules
COPY requirements.txt .
RUN pip install --no-cache-dir -r requirements.txt

# moving code to the container
COPY . .

#run the service on startup with 8 threads as well as a port
CMD exec gunicorn --bind 0.0.0.0:$PORT --workers 1 --threads 8 --
timeout 0 financeblog.wsgi:application
```

As we stated before, Docker acts similarly to a virtual machine. Think of this file like it's a set of instructions for installing a virtual machine along with some settings such as installing python, running a server etc. This is basically what we have done.

If we were to write each and every step ourself, this file would get too long. For example, we would first have to tell docker which os we want, we will then have to specify which server we want and a lot more steps. That is why we used a pre-existing image called **python:3.8-slim**. Running this command installs a version of linux along with python set up on it without us having to write those instructions ourselves.

Next we are setting a directory called "**app**" where our code will live. We are then moving the **requirements.txt** file we created earlier(it contains the required python modules for our project) to the app directory. We are then runnng the "**pip install**" command to install all the modules listed in the **requirements.txt** file. Finally we are copying our whole code to the working app directory. Lastly, we are running a service when our docker image will run. We are using gunicorn as the web server.

CLOUDMIGRATE.YML

We need a way for cloud console to run some django commands for us, for example, applyin migrations as well as run our application. For this we can create a file called **cloudmigrate.yml** which will run these commands for us. This file is used by Cloud Build to run our application. In the root of the project, create a file called **cloudmigrate.yml** and add the following code to it.

```
# [START cloudrun_django_cloudmigrate]
steps:
  - id: "build image"
    name: "gcr.io/cloud-builders/docker"
    args: ["build", "-t", "gcr.io/${PROJECT_ID}/${_SERVICE_NAME}", "."]

  - id: "push image"
```

```
    name: "gcr.io/cloud-builders/docker"
    args: ["push", "gcr.io/${PROJECT_ID}/${_SERVICE_NAME}"]

  - id: "apply migrations"
    name: "gcr.io/google-appengine/exec-wrapper"
    args:
      [
        "-i",
        "gcr.io/$PROJECT_ID/${_SERVICE_NAME}",
        "-s",
        "${PROJECT_ID}:${_REGION}:${_INSTANCE_NAME}",
        "-e",
        "SETTINGS_NAME=${_SECRET_SETTINGS_NAME}",
        "--",
        "python",
        "manage.py",
        "migrate",
      ]

  - id: "collect static"
    name: "gcr.io/google-appengine/exec-wrapper"
    args:
      [
        "-i",
        "gcr.io/$PROJECT_ID/${_SERVICE_NAME}",
        "-s",
        "${PROJECT_ID}:${_REGION}:${_INSTANCE_NAME}",
        "-e",
        "SETTINGS_NAME=${_SECRET_SETTINGS_NAME}",
        "--",
        "python",
        "manage.py",
        "collectstatic",
        "--verbosity",
        "2",
        "--no-input"
      ]
substitutions:
  _INSTANCE_NAME: django-3-postgres-instance
  _REGION: us-central1
  _SERVICE_NAME: blog-service
  _SECRET_SETTINGS_NAME: django_settings

images:
  - "gcr.io/${PROJECT_ID}/${_SERVICE_NAME}"
# [END cloudrun_django_cloudmigrate]
```

A **cloudmigrate.yml** file consists of steps of instructions that we will run. Let's look at the first instruction

```
- id: "build image"
    name: "gcr.io/cloud-builders/docker"
    args: ["build", "-t", "gcr.io/${PROJECT_ID}/${_SERVICE_NAME}", "."]
```

We have given each instruction an id. The name field points to pre-made containers available on google cloud, also called Cloud Builders, to run our build configuration. In this comand, we are using the docker cloud builder to build our local container.

```
id: "push image"
    name: "gcr.io/cloud-builders/docker"
    args: ["push", "gcr.io/${PROJECT_ID}/${_SERVICE_NAME}"]
```

This next step will push our built container to Container Registry on Cloud console.

```
id: "apply migrations"
    name: "gcr.io/google-appengine/exec-wrapper"
    args:
      [
        "-i",
        "gcr.io/$PROJECT_ID/${_SERVICE_NAME}",
        "-s",
        "${PROJECT_ID}:${_REGION}:${_INSTANCE_NAME}",
        "-e",
        "SETTINGS_NAME=${_SECRET_SETTINGS_NAME}",
        "--",
        "python",
        "manage.py",
        "migrate",
      ]
```

This step is self explanatory, we are running our migrations.

```
id: "collect static"
    name: "gcr.io/google-appengine/exec-wrapper"
    args:
      [
        "-i",
        "gcr.io/$PROJECT_ID/${_SERVICE_NAME}",
        "-s",
        "${PROJECT_ID}:${_REGION}:${_INSTANCE_NAME}",
        "-e",
        "SETTINGS_NAME=${_SECRET_SETTINGS_NAME}",
        "--",
        "python",
        "manage.py",
        "collectstatic",
```

```
        "--verbosity",
        "2",
        "--no-input"
     ]
```

And lastly, we are running the collectstatic command. This command will be new to you but the idea behind this command is to copy all of the static assets used in your project (images, css and js files) and put them in your storage location (in our case this is cloud storage bucket.).

```
substitutions:
  _INSTANCE_NAME: django-3-postgres-instance
  _REGION: us-central1
  _SERVICE_NAME: blog-service
  _SECRET_SETTINGS_NAME: django_settings
```

Lastly, in this section we have defined some variables. We used these variables throughout the file. Cloud console provides a number of environment variables to the **cloudmigrate.yml** including the **PROJECT_ID** (you can see that we didn't define it but still used it in this file) variable but it doesn't provide every information we need which is why we created some of our own variables.

Note the following:

- **_INSTANCE_NAME:** refers to the name of our database instance. Not that I am not talking about database, but database instance.
- **_REGION:** This settings determines where our service will be hosted. It will still be accessible from anywhere in the world though. Keep it as it is.
- **_SERVICE_NAME:** This is the name we want to give our running application. I've called mine **blog-serivce,** you can name it whatever you want but keep it in mind as you'll have to use it in the near future.
- **_SECRET_SETTINGS_NAME:** This is the name of the secret where we stored our **.env** file.

DEPLOYING THE DJANGO APP

Now our code is ready to be deployed. Now head over to the root of your project directory and run this command (Make sure you put your database instance name in the highligted text):

```
gcloud builds submit --config cloudmigrate.yaml --substitutions _INSTANCE_NAME=django-3-
postgres-instance,_REGION=us-central1
```

Running this command will build our docker container, run migrations and collect static assets into the cloud storage bucket. This will also push our built container to Cloud Registry. You will see a number of messages logged to your console as shown below.

Now that our Docker container is built and available on cloud console, run the following command to deploy Cloud Run service.

```
gcloud run deploy <service_name_specified_in_cloudmigrate.yml_file> --platform managed --
region us-central1 --image gcr.io/<project_id>/<service_name> --add-cloudsql-instances
<project_id>:us-central1:<database_instance_name> --allow-unauthenticated
```

Make note of the highlighted content. Put your project's values inside the highlighted content. My command looks like this:

```
gcloud run deploy blog-service --platform managed --region us-central1 --image
gcr.io/django-3-307211/blog-service --add-cloudsql-instances django-3-307211:us-
central1:django-3-postgres-instance --allow-unauthenticated
```

Running this command, you're code will be deployed as a cloud run service and if everything goes successfull, you'll receive a success message and a url link to your deployed service. I received the link https://blog-service-tksu6kd5hq-uc.a.run.app.

For security concerns, you should first head over to the django admin panel and login using the credentials we specified in our migrations file. If you remember, we called our user "**admin**". The password for this user is stored in the superuser_password secret stored in secret manager. Use these credentials to log in and create a new user.

ATTACHING A DOMAIN

Our code is live and our application works perfectly.The only thing left is to hook it up to a domain name. We are assuming that you have already bought a domain. We bought Our domain from Google Domains and have already linked it to our cloud project. Head over to https://console.cloud.google.com/run/domains

You should be taken to this screen. Make sure you are under the correct project by looking at the dropdown in the navgiation bar. Click the Add Mapping button. In the first dropdown, select our cloud run service that we deployed earlier. I named my service **blog-service** so I will select that. Next it will create another field between the two fields and ask you to verify your domain name.

Next, enter your domain name and it will ask you verify your domain.

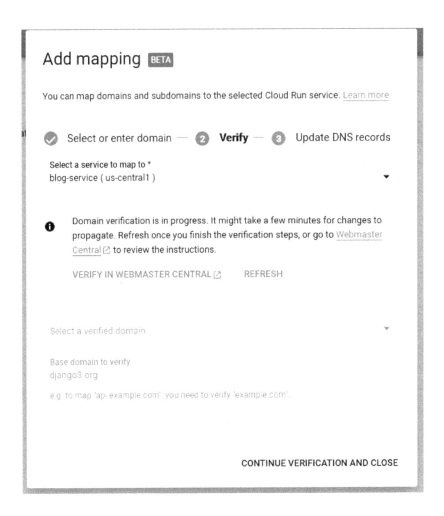

Next click the "**VERIFY IN WEBMASTER CENTRAL**" link and it will take you to the following page:

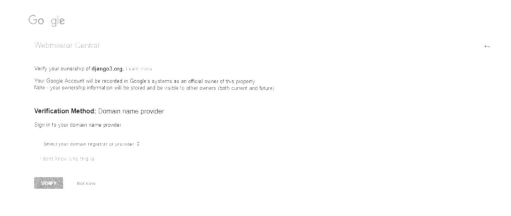

From the dropdown, select your domain registrar. Mine is Google Domains so I selected that. It will give you a string and you have to update your domain's DNS record with the given string.

Copy this string and put it in the DNS records of your domain. The name of the page on your domain registrar's website may be something like **DNS, Name Server Management, or Control Panel.**

Since I'm using Google Domain, I'll show you my steps. For google domains, head over to https://domains.google.com/registrar/**<your_domain_name_here>**. So for me it becomes. https://domains.google.com/registrar/django3.org

Then head over to the DNS page and scroll down to the very bottom to the following section. In the first field, where it says **Name**, leave it empty. It will be **@** by default. If your registrar is different, this field might be called **Host** or **Alias**. Next, select **TXT** as the type. In the **TTL** field, leave it set to default. In my case it is 1 hour. Lastly in the data field, enter the value you copied earlier from web master.

Custom resource records

Resource records define how your domain behaves. Common uses include pointing your domain at your web server or configuring email delivery for your domain. Learn more

Hit add. Go back to the webmaster page from where you copied the string and click the verify button. It might give you an error saying it wasn't able to verify your domain but wait a few minutes and try again. Now head back to the page where we were adding our custom mapping and hit the refresh button.

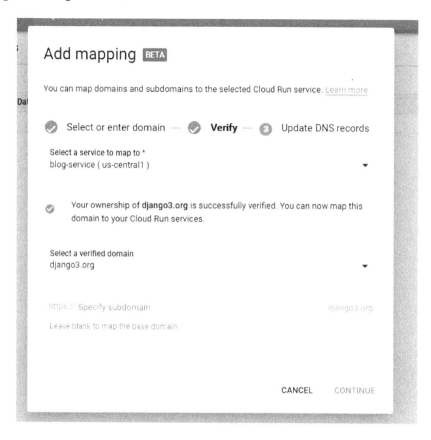

As you can see, it says it was verified successfully. Leave the subdomain field as blank and press continue. Next it will show you the following content.

You need to update the DNS records on your domain with the records provided. In case of Google Domain, you need to head back to the same page where you added the verification string. Add the records here. After adding the records, my DNS page becomes like so.

Custom resource records

Resource records define how your domain behaves. Common uses include pointing your domain at your web server or configuring email delivery for your domain. Learn more

Now head back to the custom mapping page hit done.

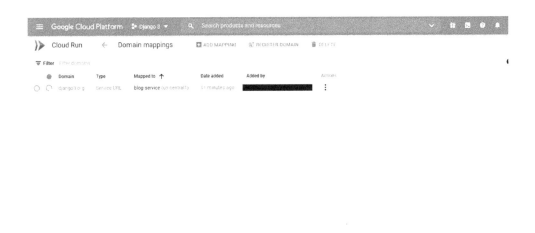

Now you just need to wait for around 48 or so hours and you'll be able to access your web application through the domain https://django3.org.

Finally, you've made it! You are a queen/king/they! Now, there is abosutely nothing between you and your dream Application! Below, you will find some basic questions related to what we've learned so far. Feel free to reach out to me on LinkedIn!

QUIZ

QUESTION 1

You have the following django template:

```
<!DOCTYPE html>
<html lang="en">
<head>
    <link rel="stylesheet" href="{% static 'main.css' %}">
    <title>Document</title>
</head>
<body>
    <h1>Hello</h1>
</body>
</html>
```

For some reason, my template is not loading the styles. Just looking at the template, can you tell what might be the cause?

QUESTION 2

Which of the following settings define the path for user uploaded images?

1. STATIC_URL
2. MEDIA_URL
3. STATICFILES_DIRS
4. MEDIA_ROOT

QUESTION 3

Considering I'm passing a path, view, and a name to the following URL pattern, can you tell what is wrong with it?

```
path("home/", views.home, "home-view")
```

QUESTION 4

What is wrong with the following class-based view?

```
class ArticleListView(generics.ListView):
    ordering = ['-published_date']
    paginate_by = 3
```

QUESTION 5

Suppose I have the following model:

```
class Comment(models.Model):
    content = models.TextField()
    user = models.ForeignKey(User, on_delete=models.CASCADE)
    is_approved = models.BooleanField()
```

Which of the following will return all the instances of Comment whose **is_approved** attribute is True?

1. `Comment.objects.all(is_aprproved=True)`
2. `Comment.objects.get(is_approved=True)`
3. `Comment.objects.filter(is_approved=True)`
4. `Comments.filter(is_approved=True)`

QUESTION 6

Considering you are in the root direcotry of a Django project,which of the following commands will create a superuser?

1. `python manage.py addsuperuser`
2. `python manage.py createadmin`
3. `python manage.py createsuperuser`
4. `python manage.py createadmin`

QUESTION 7

Consider the following code.

```
class Account(models.Model):
    story = models.TextField()
    user = models.ForeignKey(User, on_delete=models.CASCADE)

@receiver(post_save, sender=User)
def random_function(sender, instance, created, **kwargs):
    if created:
        Account.objects.create(user=instance)
```

What does the random_function function do?

1. When a User instance is created, random_function function creates an instance of Account and assigns it the newly created User.
2. When a User instance is created, random_function function updates an instance of Account by assigning it the newly created User.
3. When a User instance is updated, random_function function creates an instance of Account and assign it the updated User.
4. When a User instance is updated, random_function function updates an instance of Account by assigning it the updated created User.

QUESTION 8

Considering I have an application called **shop**, it has the following templates directory structure:

```
templates/
  shop/
    tech/
      shop_tech_list.html
    shop_cart.html
```

Considering I have some view inside my **shop** application, what path should I pass the view to display the **shop_tech_list.html**?

1. "tech/shop_tech_list.html"
2. "shop_tech_list.html"
3. "templates/shop/tech/shop_tech_list.html"
4. "shop/tech/shop_tech_list.html"

QUESTION 9

Considering I have a model called **Patient**, which of the following code snippet will make it available on Django's admin site?

1. admin.register(Patient)
2. admin.site.add(Patient)
3. admin.Site.add(Patient)
4. admin.site.register(Patient)

QUESTION 10

Which of the following will send a success flash message?

1. messages(request, "A flash message")
2. messages.success(request, "A flash message")

3. `messages.success("A flash message")`
4. `messages("A flash message")`

SOLUTIONS

QUESTION 1

The template is missing the **{% load_static %}** template tag which is why **{% static 'main.css' %}** is not working.

QUESTION 2

MEDIA_ROOT

QUESTION 3

The name of the URL has to be passed through the named parameter "**named**".

```
path("home/", views.home, name="home-view")
```

SOLUTION 4

The view is missing the required **model** parameter. Correct view would be something list this:

```
class ArticleListView(generics.ListView):
    model = Article
    ordering = ['-published_date']
    paginate_by = 3
```

SOLUTION 5:

```
Comment.objects.filter(is_approved=True)
```

SOLUTION 6:

```
python manage.py createsuperuser
```

SOLUTION 7:

When a User instance is created, **random_function** funciton creates an instance of Account and assigns it the newly created User.

SOLUTION 8:

```
"shop/tech/shop_tech_list.html"
```

SOLUTION 9:

```
admin.site.register(Patient)
```

SOLUTION 10:

```
messages.success(request, "A flash message")
```

BIBLIOGRAPHY

1. https://docs.djangoproject.com/en/3.1/faq/general/#django-appears-to-be-a-mvc-framework-but-you-call-the-controller-the-view-and-the-view-the-template-how-come-you-don-t-use-the-standard-names
2. https://www.enterprisedb.com/downloads/postgres-postgresql-downloads
3. https://docs.djangoproject.com/en/3.1/topics/settings/
4. https://docs.djangoproject.com/en/3.1/ref/models/fields/
5. https://docs.djangoproject.com/en/3.1/topics/migrations/
6. https://docs.djangoproject.com/en/3.1/topics/auth/default/
7. https://docs.djangoproject.com/en/3.1/ref/contrib/admin/
8. https://docs.djangoproject.com/en/3.1/topics/db/queries/
9. https://docs.djangoproject.com/en/3.1/topics/templates
10. https://docs.djangoproject.com/en/3.1/howto/static-files/
11. https://docs.djangoproject.com/en/3.1/howto/static-files/deployment/
12. https://docs.djangoproject.com/en/3.1/topics/signals/
13. https://docs.djangoproject.com/en/3.1/topics/forms/
14. https://docs.djangoproject.com/en/3.1/ref/contrib/messages
15. https://docs.djangoproject.com/en/3.1/topics/email/
16. https://docs.djangoproject.com/en/3.1/topics/class-based-views/generic-display/
17. https://docs.djangoproject.com/en/3.1/topics/class-based-views/mixins/
18. https://www.django-rest-framework.org/api-guide/serializers/
19. https://www.django-rest-framework.org/api-guide/authentication/
20. https://www.enterprisedb.com/postgres-tutorials/how-install-postgres-docker
21. https://docs.python.org/3/whatsnew/3.9.html
22. https://docs.python.org/3/installing/index.html
23. https://cloud.google.com/python/django/run
24. https://codelabs.developers.google.com/codelabs/cloud-run-django
25. https://cloud.google.com/run/docs/mapping-custom-domains

26. https://docs.python.org/3/library/datatypes.html
27. https://www.python.org/dev/peps/pep-0008/

CODE CONTENTS

FIGURE CONTENTS

TABLE CONTENTS